# Thinking Parent, Thinking Child

## How to Turn Your Most Challenging Everyday Problems into Solutions

### Myrna B. Shure

**RESEARCH PRESS**
PUBLISHERS

2612 North Mattis Avenue ■ Champaign, Illinois 61822 ■ (800) 519-2707
www.researchpress.com

**RESEARCH PRESS**
PUBLISHERS

Copyright © 2005 by Myrna B. Shure

5   4   3   2   1       12   13   14   15   16

Originally published under the same title by McGraw-Hill.
All rights reserved. Printed in the United States of America.

Copies of this book may be ordered from Research Press at the address given on the title page.

Composition by Jeff Helgesen
Illustrations by Carol Prichett Nagao
Cover design by Linda Brown, Positive I.D. Graphic Design, Inc.
Printed by Seaway Printing Co.

ISBN: 978-0-87822-669-6
Library of Congress Control Number 2011941183

*To all the parents and children who taught me more than I*
*could ever have taught them*

# Contents

# Part 2 ▪ Handling and Preventing Problems  73

## Part 3 ▪ Nurturing Relationships 149

## Part 4 ▪ Building Life Skills  185

# Acknowledgments

Without George Spivack, my friend and colleague for more than thirty years, the research that formed the basis of the problem-solving approach described in this book would never have been born. Funding by the Prevention Research Branch, National Institute of Mental Health, provided George and me the opportunity to identify thinking skills associated with healthy social adjustment in children aged four to twelve. This funding also enabled me to create the "I Can Problem Solve" (ICPS) program to test a new way to guide behavior—the program that laid the foundation for my work with parents.

After the publication of my first book for parents, *Raising a Thinking Child*, Ellen Foley, managing editor of the *Philadelphia Daily News*, recognized the potential for applying my problem-solving approach to a wider variety of situations—as a newspaper column that contained parenting tips. Thanks also go to Nessa Forman, vice president of corporate communications and public affairs at WHYY-FM (local NPR in Philadelphia), Kingsley Smith, then program manager, and Roger Mitchell, then vice president of educational services, for the opportunity to offer these tips on the air. It was the combination of response to the newspaper and radio parenting tips, and questions from readers of my earlier books, that provided the springboard for *Thinking Parent, Thinking Child*.

I thank Rosalie Lampson and Lisa Spector, social workers from New Albany, Ohio, for providing the quotes in the introduction. After first applying the problem-solving approach with their own children, Rosalie and Lisa now offer workshops for parents.

I am also indebted to other professionals, whom I met as I traveled the country presenting workshops that have kept my problem-solving approach alive—and who, like Rosalie and Lisa, are ICPS trainers now offering workshops of their own for families and for schools. The insights and experiences of these trainers stimulated my thinking and inspired parts of this book. These individuals are Bonnie Aberson, Psy.D., neuropsychologist and school psychologist, Dade County, Florida; Dee Austin, Ed.D., parent specialist, Rogers, Arkansas; Phyllis Bullock-Beaufait, M.A., school counselor, Dorothy L. Bullock School, Glassboro, New Jersey; Alberto Bustoz, violence prevention specialist, Metropolitan Family Services, Chicago, Illinois; Ruth Cross, M.A., Principal, Mill Street School, Naperville, Illinois; Nonie Downing, M.S., parent mentor coordinator, NCO Youth and Family Services, Naperville, Illinois; Kathleen Krol, Ph.D., school counselor, Lincoln Park School, Lincoln Park, New Jersey; Jane Mc-Gaugh, Ed.S., prevention specialist, I Care Program, Baton Rouge, Louisiana; Robin Nelson, M.A., instructional support team, Governor Mifflin School District, Shillington, Pennsylvania; Merrick O'Connell, M.S.W., social services manager, El Valor Early Childhood Center, Chicago, Illinois; Dawn Oparah, M.A., educational consultant, Amadi Leadership Associates, Atlanta, Georgia; Kathleen Piede, prevention specialist, St. Mary's School, Schwenksville, Pennsylvania; Michelle Scheidt, project director, Metropolitan Family Services, Chicago, Illinois; Rebecca Smith-Andoh, M.S.W., social worker, Mill Street School, Naperville, Illinois; Richard Titus, Director, New Jersey Child Care Training Program, EIRC, Sewell, New Jersey; and educational consultants in private practice: Heidi De-Staven, L.C.S.W., Freehold, New Jersey; Lynne Devine, Houston, Texas; Kristin Funk, L.C.S.W., Eugene, Oregon; Ann-Linn Glaser, Moorestown, New Jersey; Louise Krikorian, M.S., New York, New York; Lisa Lakner, Houston, Texas; Mary Kate Land, Garden Grove, California; Sandra Sheard, M.A., Folsom, New Jersey; Mary Beth Willis, M.S.W., Bear, Delaware; and Monique Winslow, Ph.D., Raleigh, North Carolina.

I also acknowledge Ann Wendel, former president of Research Press, for permission to include the silly skit in Chapter 16 from my "I Can Problem Solve" curriculum for schools. In addition, the quotes introducing each of the four parts of this book originally appeared in my recent book, *Raising a Thinking Preteen*, published by Henry Holt.

My agent, Lynn Seligman, believed in my work from the beginning. I have known Lynn now for almost ten years, and I thank her for encouraging me to continue expanding my problem-solving approach in new ways.

I also thank Lynn for introducing me to Roberta Israeloff, who not only kept me calm in the face of tight deadlines but helped me write this book with the same sensitivity and insights that she did with *Raising a Thinking Preteen*.

Judith McCarthy, my editor at McGraw-Hill, publisher of the first edition of this book, added invaluable insights as she used the problem-solving approach with her own children. In fact, some of her thought-provoking anecdotes are included in this book. A special tribute goes to Gail Salyards, President of Research Press, for her continued support of the *I Can Problem Solve* series for schools, the *Raising a Thinking Child Workbook* for parents, and now for recognizing the value of adding *Thinking Parent, Thinking Child* to the Research Press family. Appreciation is also expressed to Karen Steiner, the editor for the *I Can Problem Solve* series, and now for this book, for her meticulous attention to detail, giving this book new, important finishing touches.

Gerald Bello, Ph.D., my friend and associate professor, College of Nursing and Health Professions at Drexel University, not only gave me emotional support throughout but contributed significantly to the creation of some of the entries. My uncle, Harold Laufman, M.D., patiently listened to some of the anecdotes, and in his infinite wisdom suggested ways to express them—some of which appear on the pages in this book. And my good friend Barry Brait inspired me to think about new ways that everyday events can, as he put it, "allow doors to open for discussion about what's important in our lives."

But most of all, it was parents and kids who are at the heart of *Thinking Parent, Thinking Child*. I express my gratitude to the hundreds of families with children aged four to twelve who served as a basis for the incidents I chose to include. While those who participated in my research must remain anonymous, I would like to acknowledge by name others who contributed immeasurably by talking with me, sometimes for hours, or for giving me the opportunity to watch their children in play. (In the book, all of their names have been changed, with the exception of Montel Williams, syndicated talk-show host.) Some of the stories were provided by parents, grandparents, or caregivers; some by parents and their children; and some by children who shared their thoughts and stories out of earshot of adults.

Parents, grandparents, and caregivers include Stephanie Brooks, M. J. Czerpak, Connie Garcia, Marion Gillespie, Cindy Handler, Kirk Heilbrun, James Herbert, Christi Hetrick, Dorothy Hochman, Sherry Hopkins, George Johnson, Kathy Kane, Rose Keane, Dov Leis, Robin Lewis, Cheryl Litzke, John Makransky, Paul Nolan, Frank Roberts, Joan Roll, Stephanie Shore, Barbara Skypala-Conway, Roxane Staley, Janet Stern, and J. Michael Williams.

Parents and their children who also contributed include Bruce and Linda Boguslav, and Mayla and Arielle; Lisa Hoffstein, and Hillary; Joe McCaffrey, and Kaitlyn; Judith Mercuris, and Sophie; Elizabeth Robinson, and Jimmy and Gregory; and Jonathan Silberg, and Sarah.

Among other youngsters I spoke with or observed in play are John Breslin, Francesca and Giovanna Chiabella, Elizabeth Conarroe, Alex and Matt Domenick, Yianni Eleftheriou, Elliott and Sylvia Herbert, Mathew Hyman, Enrique Inclan, Aliza Kahn, Michael Katz, Gabriela Laufman Kogut, Kaley Laren, Akia Malone, Benjamin Olsho, Margo Schoenberg, Alexi Several, Joshua Thomas, and Gabrielle Weiss.

Without shared, personal stories, this book would not have been possible.

# A Message for You

*Tell me, I forget.*
*Teach me, I remember.*
*Involve me, I understand.*
—Chinese proverb

It's eight o'clock in the morning. You hear the school bus rumbling up the block, and your seven-year-old has not even begun getting dressed.

Your four-year-old returns from a playdate in tears. "Tommy hit me," she sobs, "and broke my new toy."

An important client calls you at home, and in the middle of your conversation, your six-year-old asks you—loudly—to help find his shoes even though you've told him a hundred times not to interrupt you on the phone.

Three days before Easter, your nine-year-old announces that she's not going with you to visit relatives on Sunday.

"My teacher said I cheated on a test, but I didn't!" cries your indignant eleven-year-old.

How often do your kids argue over toys, computer time, video games, or other possessions? How frequently do they fight—with you, with each other—over anything or everything? How often do they create tension in the house because they don't listen, won't do what you want, and talk back? Do you feel as if you've tried everything and nothing's worked?

If you're looking for a different way to handle situations like these, this book is for you. My thirty-plus years of research with families and in schools shows that children who can think through and successfully solve everyday problems for themselves have fewer behavior problems and do better in school than children who are unable to think this way.

In my two earlier books, *Raising a Thinking Child* and *Raising a Thinking Preteen*, I introduced and explained a practical, step-by-step program designed to teach children critical-thinking skills, which I call the "I Can Problem Solve" program, or ICPS for short. This program describes specific games, activities, and dialogues parents can use to teach their children to respond more thoughtfully and resourcefully to problems and conflicts that arise in the course of daily living.

I've received thousands of touching letters, e-mails, and phone calls from parents who have tried my ICPS program with their children. Some parents appreciated the fact that the program was consistent and respectful, as this mother did:

> *The book* Raising a Thinking Child *has been like a gift for our family. Our six-year-old has blossomed into a very feeling problem solver who seems to have a strong sense of who she is and what she thinks. As parents, my husband and I feel we now have a parenting approach that is calm and respectful to guide our children to handle the problems in their lives from sharing, to peer pressure, and well beyond into adulthood. Our family thanks Dr. Shure for her wonderful contribution to the parenting literature.*

Another parent focused on specific aspects of the ICPS program:

> *More conflicts have been resolved by my children because I shifted focus. My consistent use of the dialoguing technique Dr. Shure has developed shifted the responsibility of solving most of their daily problems from me to my children.*

This mother realized that the "dialoguing technique" that I created was at the heart of my problem-solving approach. What do I mean by this technique?

Let's say, for example, that four-year-old Patty and her eight-year-old sister Val were arguing over a clay set that their aunt gave Patty for her birthday. Patty defiantly informed her sister that the clay was hers, and

Val couldn't play with it. Within minutes, the girls were screaming at each other so loudly that their mother Julia knew she had to intervene.

Here is how Patty and Val's mother used the "dialogue technique" to help her daughters resolve their conflict so the girls would end up satisfied with the solution.

**Mom:** What's the matter? What's the problem?
**Patty:** It's my clay, and Val is taking it all.
  **Val:** I just want a little bit. Patty never shares anything, and I always share my things with her.
**Mom:** Patty, you're both yelling at each other. How are you feeling now?
**Patty:** Mad!
**Mom:** Val, how are you feeling?
  **Val:** I'm mad! Patty is so selfish! She never shares!
**Mom:** Yelling at each other is one way to deal with this problem. What's happening now?
**Patty:** We're fighting.
**Mom:** Can you two think of a *different* way to solve this problem so you both won't be mad and you won't fight?
  **Val:** She can have the red clay and I can have the blue clay, and then we can take turns.
**Mom:** Patty, is that a good idea?
**Patty:** Yeah, I can make a cake and she can have it for dessert.
  **Val:** OK, and I'll make the frosting.

As you can see, Julia doesn't talk *at* her daughters, but instead asks questions. This technique not only directly involves children in the process of solving their own problems, but it also enables Julia to find out what the problem *is* from her children's perspectives. It also gives Val the opportunity to express her feelings—that she is particularly upset because she believes that she routinely shares her things with Patty and Patty doesn't reciprocate.

It's also important to note that each question Julia asks has a specific purpose. When, for instance, she asks her daughters how they are feeling, she's helping her children develop a sense of empathy. One reason why empathy is important is that we can't care about how others feel until we learn to care about our own feelings. When Julia asks, "What's happening now?" the children are asked to consider the consequences of their behavior. Finally, to help her children come up with their own solution to the problem, she asks, "Can you two think of a *different* way to solve this problem so you both won't be mad and you won't fight?"

*Different* is a key word in the dialogue technique. In fact, you will see in several chapters in this book a series of words that I've italicized to indicate that they are being used in a new way. Other words—such as *not*, *before*, and *after*—also become key words when used, for example, in the following questions: "Is your idea a good one or *not* a good one?" "What happened *before* you hit him?" "What happened *after*?"

When children think about these questions, using these and other key words, something unique happens. Instead of walking away feeling angry, frustrated, bored, or overpowered, children feel empowered, and are more likely to be satisfied with the solutions. As my research has shown, children are much more likely to carry out their own solutions than those that parents might think are best.

How does this problem-solving approach differ from other ways that parents might handle problems that come up with their children? Let's go back to the situation with Julia's angry daughters, and suppose that she had used what psychologists call power assertion, which I simply call the power approach. She would have said something like, "Give me that clay. If you two can't share, I'll put it away and neither of you can have it!" Or, "I don't want to hear any more yelling. Patricia! Don't be so selfish!" Techniques such as yelling, demanding, depriving kids of what they want, and even resorting to the time-honored time-out may bring about the desired result—which is to stop the fighting—but parents may only feel satisfied in the short run.

That's because the power approach overlooks one extremely important part of the picture: the children themselves. How do *they* feel? Very likely, they are still as angry and frustrated as they were when the fight began. Not only that, but they haven't learned how to solve their problem, which could easily mean that as soon as the time-out is over, they'll argue over the clay set again. And tomorrow, they'll just as easily argue over something else. Another pitfall of relying on the power approach is that, over time, children begin to feel so overpowered that they may become indifferent or resentful and, as a result, may vent their frustration on other friends, or at school.

Other strategies Julia could have used are what I call the suggesting approach and the explaining approach. If Julia had used the suggesting approach, she would have told her children what *to* do instead of what *not* to do. For example, she would have said, "You should ask for what you want," or "You should share your toys." Had she taken the explaining approach, she would have said something like, "If you two don't learn to share, no one will play with you, and you won't have any friends." This approach operates under the assumption that children who understand the impact of their behavior are less likely to engage in behaviors that would hurt themselves or others. As part of the explaining approach, Julia might have relied on the widely used "I" message, such as, "*I* feel angry when you two argue like that."

While suggesting and explaining are more positive than the power approach, parents who use these three approaches are still thinking *for* their children. Instead of asking their children to solve problems themselves, these parents engage in a one-way monologue. These parents are talking *to*, not *with*, their children, and, in all likelihood, their children have already tuned out any suggestions or explanations their parents have to offer. Moreover, parents end up exasperated because their children aren't listening to them—which in turn results in a no-win situation for everybody.

Indeed, none of these three approaches encourages parents to recognize or understand their children's feelings; nor do these approaches address the parents' feelings when they are facing tense situations with their children.

Using the dialogue technique as a problem-solving approach—the approach that Julia actually used with her daughters—addresses both the parents' and their children's needs and vulnerabilities. The result is a win-win situation.

Julia knows this. She's a *thinking* parent.

The essence of being a thinking parent is to be proactive, not reactive. Whether your child is entangled in a problem with siblings, classmates, friends, or with you, the thinking parent weighs options, decides how to respond, and helps children figure out *how* to think, not *what* to think, so that their children can solve problems for themselves.

Now let's consider three children, all aged five, who wanted to play with a cherished toy.

Lenny said to his younger brother, "Give me that train! It's mine and it's my turn." When his brother refused, Lenny grabbed the toy and left the room.

Sonja asked her sister for a turn to play with her doll. When her sister refused, Sonja gave up, left the room, and sulked.

Anthony asked his brother for a turn with his truck. When Anthony was refused, he asked, "Why can't I have it?"

"I need it, I'm putting out a fire," his brother said.

"I can be your helper," Anthony countered. "I'll get a hose and we can put the fire out together."

How does Anthony differ from Lenny and Sonja? Lenny reacted to frustration by acting out, in this case by grabbing the toy. Sonja ventured one suggestion—to have a turn playing with the doll—but when her sister refused, she gave up and retreated.

Anthony did neither. When he realized that his first solution didn't work, he came up with another. While Anthony may have thought of hitting his brother or grabbing the truck, he didn't. His sense of empathy wouldn't let him. Instead, he found ways to negotiate for what he wanted without hurting himself or his brother. He was able to take both their needs into account.

Anthony is a *thinking* child.

All children can be taught to think as Anthony does. Not only does the ability to problem-solve have a lasting impact on what children do now, but, as my research shows, this ability also profoundly impacts what they might do later—such as resisting peer pressure to engage in more potentially damaging behavior like experimenting with drugs, alcohol, unsafe sex, and violence.

And further down the road, the thinking child will likely grow up to be a thinking parent.

My goal in writing *Thinking Parent, Thinking Child* is to offer an easy-to-read compendium of challenging everyday problems facing parents and their children from preschool through the preteen years—complete with hands-on tools for turning those problems into solutions.

The book is organized thematically. Each chapter focuses on a particular issue—like anger, aggression, or empathy—and includes several different vignettes reflecting those issues. This organization allows you to consider each topic from a variety of perspectives.

In this book, you'll learn ways to give your child the skills to make sound decisions, as well as the freedom to use these new skills. You will learn to guide your children to change their behavior to become less aggressive, inhibited, and fearful; more cooperative and empathic; and better able to adjust to and cope with life's frustrations and disappointments. You will also see how problem-solving skills can help children do better academically. And you will watch as they become more genuinely empathic. Thanks to the problem-solving approach, children will come to appreciate that parents have feelings, too.

Some chapters will encourage you to reflect on your own behavior toward your child. They will ask you stimulating questions: How really useful are time-outs? Will spanking help or hurt my child? What do we do when I think one way about an issue and my spouse thinks the opposite? Do I need to become a better listener? How can I do this? What message might I be sending my child if I don't keep my promises?

As you use this book, you will not only gain confidence in handling everyday situations, but you will also learn how to engage your children on a daily basis in the dialogue techniques of problem solving. And you'll be helping to ensure that your children have the tools they need to cope with life not just today, but next year, and ten years later, as well as on into adulthood. Even if you're already familiar with the ICPS program from my earlier books, you'll find *Thinking Parent, Thinking Child* an invaluable and easy reference to use when specific problems occur—as they inevitably will.

Though I believe in the usefulness and effectiveness of my approach, I also never say "never" to any parenting technique. For example, I would never advise you never to yell at a child or never to show your anger. That would be unnatural. We all need to vent our feelings, and children have to learn to cope with that reality. However, if you always—or even mostly—react by becoming angry and doling out punishment when your kids do something you don't want them to do, it will be more difficult for them to become independent, thinking children. While I don't tell you what to do, I give you new ways to look at issues to help you decide what's best for you and your family.

Researcher Irving Sigel of the Educational Testing Service in Princeton, New Jersey, told me (in November 2000), "Each time one teaches a child something he could have discovered for himself, the child is kept from inventing it, and consequently, from understanding it completely." My hope is that this book will help you give your children this opportunity to discover how to navigate—and understand—their interpersonal worlds.

And where better can a child learn to think this way than at home? As Bonnie Aberson, a neuropsychologist and school psychologist who has been practicing the ICPS program for more than fifteen years, has said, "Children can learn that no matter how difficult situations may be in other settings, the family will provide a sanctuary where everyone is heard and accepted, and problems can be solved. It is the open and accepting communication fostered by ICPS that increases the bonding and feelings of empowerment that problems can, indeed, be solved."

While it is never too late to start, it's also never too early.

What we're really saying to our kids is, "I care how you feel, I care what you think, and I want you to care, too." We are also affirming, "I trust you to make good decisions." After trying the problem-solving approach described in *Thinking Parent, Thinking Child*, I believe you will feel safe in granting that trust.

■

# PART 1

# Dealing with Feelings

*Children who can take control of their lives*
*will not let life take control of them.*

The moment your daughter walks in the door after school you know that something wonderful has happened to her—you can read her happiness in her eyes, her walk, even her posture. "Mommy!" she cries, so delighted that she can scarcely get the words out—"Remember that book report I had to write? I got it back today and my teacher loved it. I got an A!"

Happiness like this is often contagious. You know just how to respond: "That's wonderful news! I'm so happy for you!"

Other days, your daughter's feelings may be harder to read. Her eyes are guarded, and she doesn't say much. You wonder what questions would help her open up—and then wonder if she would even want to talk. If you press her, she may become frustrated and close up even more.

Some days, she may come home looking downright miserable. "Jamie said I wasn't her best friend anymore," she says when asked, her voice so weak you can barely hear her.

What do you say now? How can you help her to feel better?

Feelings are not only universal but also present at birth—just watch a hungry infant being fed and notice the kaleidoscope of emotions that play on his face as he registers anger, frustration, surprise, satisfaction, and happiness. But few things are as hard to manage as feelings.

Although feelings are ineffable—we can't touch or smell them— they are undeniably real. And they also have a physical component. We tend to feel emotions in our bodies. Some of us feel fear in the pit of our stomachs; some in the back of our throats. We all have different reactions.

The first step toward helping your child deal with her feelings is to deal with your own. You can begin by becoming aware of your own emotional responses to events in your life. How do you feel when something wonderful happens, such as getting a promotion at work?

Now think about this. How do you feel when you want something to happen and then it doesn't? How do you feel when something you thought *would* happen, doesn't? Do you fly off the handle, feel frustrated or sad? Do you take it out on others, give up, or find a way to make things better?

Once you've identified your own feelings and your reactions to them, you can help your child identify hers. Children learn about feelings from us. When we experience happiness, for instance, or see it in our kids, we name it—"You look so happy today!" "Why do you look so sad?" Over time, children learn to associate the feeling inside with the word.

Naming emotions is a powerful tool. Children feel more in control of themselves and their world when they can describe how they're feeling. That's why it's important to help children to recognize the full range of emotions. Many kids, when asked how they feel, say things like, "good," "terrific," "bad," "awful," or "terrible." Very few answer "happy," "proud," "sad," "frustrated," "afraid." Not only does identifying a feeling word help children more clearly understand how they truly feel, but it might determine what they do next. A child might do something different if he feels sad than if he feels frustrated. Just thinking he feels "bad," "terrible," or "awful" will not help him make an informed decision about his next step.

Besides helping children learn to label and recognize their feelings, it's also important to help them feel safe to express their emotions. In my research with children, I learned that when children feel safe—and this applies to boys as much as girls—they enjoy talking about all their emotions, even the not-so-good ones.

When children become good problem solvers, they will be able to think of the potential consequences of revealing their inner thoughts and feelings. They then can make the decision whether it is safe enough to relate those thoughts and feelings to others—that is, whether they can talk to a friend about a fear they have without worrying that the conversation will come back to haunt them. This gives them a sense of power because it becomes their decision about what to say to others and what to keep to themselves.

The chapters you'll read in Part 1 illustrate ways to help your children cope with feelings that are sometimes hard to express—especially for boys—such as disappointment, frustration, sadness, and fear; and feelings like anger that at times may be difficult to control. I will also explore the more elusive and sometimes chronic feelings like stress and anxiety, whether these result from going to a new school, taking tests, emotional strains that can interfere with learning, or coping with events we can't control, such as chronic, life-threatening illness in the family. Finally, I'll consider devastating feelings like loss—when a friend moves away, when a pet dies, or when a beloved family member passes on.

You will see how learning to handle such difficult situations as these can help our children become caring, empathic human beings who can understand and accept their emotions. They will also learn that they can control their emotions. This helps them feel in control of their lives—which means that they'll be less likely to let life take control of them.

# 1

# Anger

## Oh, Those Tantrums!

You're in the grocery store with your three-year-old when he spots a box of cereal he wants. He reaches for it hungrily, but you tell him that you don't want to buy it—it's too sweet—and you select a brand with less sugar. Angry, he strains against the cart. Growing agitated, he flails his arms, his face turns red—and you get that awful, sinking feeling in the pit of your stomach. He's going to have another tantrum. He had one just the other day when you were visiting your mother. They always come at the worst possible time.

By now your son is screaming and you have to figure out what to do.

You can plead with him to stop crying, but he won't hear you. You can threaten that you won't take him to the playground when you're done, as you promised—but that doesn't faze him. You can ignore it and hope it will go away, but you know it won't. You can give in and put the box of cereal in your cart, but you don't want him to grow up thinking that he'll get his way if he cries hard enough. You can get angry in turn—raise your voice, grab the box out of his hands—but how can you expect your child to learn about controlling his temper if you don't control yours?

Unfortunately, none of these possibilities sounds appealing—or effective. There's no perfect way to deal with tantrums. But there is a way to avoid them—to stop them before they begin.

You can do it by playing the "Same and Different" game with your child.

One afternoon, when you and your child are feeling relaxed and enjoying each other's company, tell your child to watch what you do with your arms. First, make big circles with your outstretched arms. Then, clap your hands. Now ask your child, "Did I just do the *same* thing or something *different?*"

When your child replies, "Different," think of two different things you can do with your feet so that she gets the answer right again. Then ask her to make up two body motions and to ask you if she's doing the same thing or something different.

You can also play this game on the playground. "Look at those two kids," you can say. "Is their shirt the *same* color, or *different?*"

Play it when you watch television, take a car ride, or walk to a friend's house. The goal is to teach him about the words *same* and *different*.

How does this relate to tantrums? The next time you're in the store, or at your mother's, and you sense that your child is heading for a tantrum, you can calmly say to him, "Let's play the 'same and different' game. Can you think of a *different* way to tell me how you're feeling right now?"

One three-year-old stopped crying the moment her mother asked her the question. She remembered playing the game with her mother, laughed, and said, "Yeah, I can make circles with my arms." Her tantrum was history.

Another child, four years old, was on the verge of blossoming into a tantrum on the playground when her mother asked, "Can you think of a *different* way to tell me how you feel?"

The girl recognized the word *different*, paused, smirked for a moment, and calmed down. A five-year-old girl screaming for some ice cream stopped yelling when her mother asked her the same question and said, deadpan, "But ice cream will help me grow." Mom couldn't keep from laughing. Although she had to muster all her resolve to keep from giving in, she held her ground. Within a minute, her child's cries turned to laughter as well.

---

"Can you think of a *different* way to tell me how you feel?"

---

Turn tantrums into an opportunity to teach your child that he has a choice—that he can choose among a wide spectrum of possibilities to express how he is feeling. That way, you'll both stay more in control.

## Darn Those Curse Words!

Darren, age eight, came home from school one day looking sullen. "I had a fight with a kid on the bus," he said. "I hate him. He's a goddamn liar." Rosemary, his mother, had never heard him use that word before, and even though she sympathized with how he was feeling, she immediately told him never to use it again.

Later, as he talked to his friend on the phone, she heard him say, "My math teacher's such a bitch."

"Darren," she said, interrupting him. "Never use that language again! Go to your room!" He slammed the door so hard that the house shook.

That same evening, when Rosemary asked him about his science homework, he replied, "I don't know what the hell is happening in that class."

Rosemary was floored. What was happening to her son? He had never talked like that before. Sure, she knew that kids are exposed to cursing—it's in songs, movies, and even on TV. But why was he suddenly drawn to those very words she found offensive?

She told him to stop, explaining that she didn't like to hear those words. "But everybody talks like that," he said. Next, she explained that curse words make some people feel uncomfortable. "Not my friends," he replied. And when she asked him why his language had become so offensive, he shrugged and said, "Because."

Rosemary was at her wit's end. What could she do?

Rosemary thought about whether something else was upsetting him, causing him to use objectionable language. Cursing can be the result of the real problem, not the problem itself. For example, Jerome, ten, who had always been a good math student, couldn't master fractions, and was becoming very frustrated. Too proud to ask for help, he began to fail math tests. He also began cursing, especially in discussions about school. It was a way of venting his frustration. When his parents discovered the source of Jerome's problem, they were able to arrange for him to get some extra help in fractions—which not only raised his grades but stopped the cursing.

Many times, though, children like Darren use curse words for the shock value of them and to be defiant. If you suspect that this is motivating your child, you can ask,

"How do you think I feel when you talk like that?"

"Can you think of a *different* way to tell me [or your friends] how you feel?"

Darren was so surprised at being asked these questions that he was stopped in his tracks. He also came to appreciate that his mother has feelings, too. She never heard him curse again.

## "Mommy, I Hate You!"

Paul, nine, played with a friend after school, came home late, and didn't get his homework done in time. This was the second time this week Paul hadn't lived up to his school responsibilities. Fran, his mother, was very angry with him, and as he came in for dinner, she said, "If you do this again you'll be grounded for a week."

Paul felt trapped. He narrowed his eyes, his face turned red, and he spat out the words, "I hate you, Mom!"

Fran felt as if he'd punched her in the stomach. Hate is a strong word. You can't help but react to it. In her heart, Fran knew that Paul didn't really mean that he hated her—or if he did, it was only for that moment. But she couldn't deny how hurt, shocked, and angry she felt, nor could she hide her feelings from her son.

But she also knew that Paul was very angry, too, and she didn't want to ignore his feelings. This was a moment, she knew, that shouldn't pass without her saying something. But what could she say to make the situation better rather than inflame it?

If she said, "I don't hate you," he probably wouldn't hear that—and even if he did, he wouldn't care since he was still caught up in the heat of the moment.

If she tried to explain why learning to meet your responsibilities is an important part of growing up, he probably wouldn't hear that either, because he's not interested in hearing about obligations or logical reasoning right now.

She could say, "I know you're angry but you can't always do what you want." That's a better response because it would let Paul know that she understood how angry he was. But it wouldn't help him feel less frustrated and upset.

Here's how I suggest you respond when this situation unfolds at your house. Ask your child: "How do you think I feel when you talk to me like that?"

Paul was surprised when Fran asked him this question. He'd never stopped to consider how his mother felt as a result of his actions. But since he was still angry, he just shrugged and said, "I don't know."

Then Fran asked, "Can you think of a *different* way to tell me how you feel?" Still angry, Paul just walked away. But when he remembered the hurt look on his mother's face, he returned, apologized, and told her that he really didn't mean it.

Now that Fran and Paul are calmed down, Fran can address the problem that inflamed her son in the first place. She can now ask, "What can you think of to do so you will get your homework done on time?" Paul didn't have an answer to that question because he hadn't heard it before; he had to think about it. Finally, he said, "I could do my homework first and then play with my friend." (For more on helping your child plan his homework time, see Chapter 18.)

When you ask your child questions in this way, he learns that it's not his *feelings* that are a problem, but the way in which he *expressed* them. In time, Paul came to appreciate how hurtful his expression of anger could be. He also learned to think about how another person would react to his feelings. When he did feel angry, he found other ways to express it.

The more we lash out at our kids, the more they'll lash out—or want to lash out—at us.

Fran's new way of talking to her son is a far cry from threatening to ground him. And Paul didn't have to "hate" her anymore.

## Is Your Child Angry?
## What Does He Really Understand?

Men may be from Mars and women from Venus, but children, especially young children, often seem as if they're from a planet all their own.

Let me give you some examples. One morning, I walked into a pre-school classroom and, seeing a happy, enthusiastic child, I greeted him by saying, "Hi, pal."

"I'm not Pal," the child told me. "I'm Richard."

Another time, I was waiting for a taxi outside of New York City's Penn Station listening to the family behind me describing their travels from Boston to Niagara Falls and now to New York. "You're really moving around," I said, with a smile.

The six-year-old in the family turned to correct me. "We're not moving, we're just visiting," she said, very matter-of-factly, in a perfect demonstration of how concretely young children think.

At the very least, children seem to both use words more concretely and think about the world differently than we do. Perhaps that's why we often find ourselves explaining to our children what to do and why, and then getting exasperated when they don't do what we ask. What we often fail to realize is that children may genuinely not understand what we're asking of them.

Here is an example of how parents can misinterpret their child's behavior: Four-year-old Eli angrily threw his glass from the table to the floor because he wanted to go watch TV when his mom told him that he need-ed to stay at the table. When the glass shattered, his mom sent him to his room, screaming, "Don't you *ever* do that again! You can't go around breaking things! You did that on purpose and Mommy is very angry with you. Do you understand?"

Scared and dutiful, Eli said, "Yes." His mother was satisfied that he had learned his lesson.

But had he?

When I think about this situation, I'm not so sure. It seems to me that, in reality, one of three things might have happened:

- Eli really did learn his lesson, and won't throw objects anymore when he doesn't get his way.
- Eli didn't hear a word his mom said.
- Eli didn't really understand the point his mother tried to make.

The first case is unlikely. One threatening command does not change a child's behavior that quickly. The second is more likely: because Eli doesn't like to be yelled at, he probably shut out every word his mother yelled at him.

But the most likely scenario is the third. Most four-year-olds do not distinguish intent from what actually happens. That is, it's quite possible that Eli didn't understand what was so terrible about breaking one glass. Like many kids his age, he may have thought it would be naughtier to break five glasses accidentally by bumping into someone he didn't see holding a tray of five glasses than to break one on purpose because he was angry and threw the glass on the floor. Why? Because five is more than one.

The same holds true for four-year-old Megan who grabbed some clay from her friend because "Julie had more." In reality, both girls had the same amount of clay. But Julie had flattened hers into a pancake, and so it now looked larger. To Megan, it looked as though she'd been cheated.

Next time you ask your child, "Do you understand?" consider the pos-sibility that, whatever he says, he may not.

Psychologist Jean Piaget's experiments with his own children give us some games to play that will help us appreciate how children think about the concepts "more" and "less," and why we may not understand each other when we feel angry.

Place ten pennies in a row with some space in between each. Now line up ten more pennies under the first ten. Ask your child, "Do these rows have the same number of pennies or does one row have more?"

Most likely he'll answer, correctly, "The same."

Now, *while he's watching*, push the bottom row so that the pennies are more closely together and ask, "Do these rows have the same number of pennies or does one row have more?"

Now he might respond, "The top row has more." That's because it looks longer. He's focusing on what he sees and how things look—even though he saw that you didn't remove any pennies from the bottom row. To help your child see what really happened, let him push the bottom row of pennies closer together himself. Ask him if any pennies were added or taken away. Even with this, he still may not understand that the two rows have the same number of pennies until about age six or seven.

Next time your child thinks she's being cheated when you give her the same amount of clay as her friend, but one piece ends up looking larger than the other, try this: Show her two glasses of water, the same size, with the same amount of water. Ask your child if one glass has more or if they are both the same. She will probably answer correctly, "The same." Now, while she's watching, pour the water from one glass into a taller, thinner one. Now she'll probably think the taller, thinner one has more water, because "it's higher." Then pour the water from the taller, thinner glass back into the original one. Now she'll probably say they're "the same." Now roll both clumps of clay into a ball so they look the same. Now, while she's watching, roll one out flat so it looks bigger. Some children will catch on, but again, some won't until they are a little older.

We may think a child understands things the way we do, but further questioning often reveals that they have another interpretation altogether. And if we understand that young children think differently than we do, we can also better understand why they behave the way they do.

# 2

# Frustration and Disappointment

## "My Child Hates to Lose"

Your eight-year-old son and ten-year-old daughter are playing a game of checkers. When he loses, he starts crying, "She cheated!"

You suggest they play another game. This time, your daughter loses. "I let him win," she says, enraging him.

Your nine-year-old daughter begins to sabotage any game she's playing the moment she senses that she may lose. "Stop bossing me around!" she shouts to her opponent and quits.

And your twelve-year-old is so anxious about losing at anything—whether it's a card game or at the bowling alley—that he doesn't play any games at all.

There are many things you can say in this situation. You can try to become philosophical and say, "You'll win the next time"—but you can't promise that. He might not win the next time, or the time after that. And when your child can't trust you, you've lost a huge battle.

You can also say, "You'll forget about it tomorrow." But maybe she won't.

You can try to comfort your child by saying, "I'm sorry you lost. I know you feel bad." But this may end the conversation completely. When you suggest to your child how he feels, you prevent him from exploring what it is about losing that makes him feel the way he does. It's even possible that he doesn't feel bad at all; losing can mean something entirely different to him than it does to you.

Becoming a good loser is an experience of mastery. It takes time. When children don't like to lose, it's often because they don't feel good about themselves. Or they may think that something's not right. As one older brother explained to me after losing a game of chess to his younger sister, "I'm not *supposed* to lose to her." It's also possible that children who have trouble losing have an inordinate need to gain control or to feel power.

It's not that the strategies I mentioned above are harmful as much as they're ineffective. And the reason they don't work is because they don't address what's at the root of your child's problem, which isn't the fact of winning or losing but how he feels.

What can you do that's more effective?

Instead of focusing on the game or assuming how he's feeling, ask him how he's feeling. After he's talked about how he feels, turn the attention to the other person by asking, "How do you think your sister feels when you say that she won because she cheated?"

Your child may recognize that the other child might feel sad or mad. That's a good beginning.

Now ask, "Does your sister win some of the time or all of the time?"

Most likely, your child will acknowledge that his sister wins only some of the time. Then ask, "Can you think of something *different* to say to your sister so she won't feel sad or mad?"

These kinds of questions can help children understand the concept of winning and losing in the larger context of thinking about their own and others' feelings. This way, they learn to be good losers and good winners. By focusing on your child's feelings, he will accept that while it feels good to win, he is still the same person when he loses.

As W. Timothy Gallwey tells us in his classic book *The Inner Game of Tennis*, "Focus in tennis is fundamentally no different from the focus to perform any task . . . and learning to welcome obstacles in competition automatically increases one's ability to find advantages in all the difficulties one meets in the course of one's life." Gallwey also points out that winning a game is an external phenomenon; it doesn't affect or change who we are on the inside.

You can also get your child involved with an activity she can easily master—in order to feel good about herself. Perhaps your daughter wants to help you make cookies. That way, she will not only learn a new skill but also enjoy some special time alone with you.

It may take a while for children to appreciate that love and attention aren't contingent on whether they win or lose. Parents who help their children feel more self-confident will raise children who feel good about themselves and have more fun. That frees them to focus simply on the enjoyment of playing.

And, isn't learning how to lose just as important as learning how to win?

## Does Your Child Have to Be the Center of Attention?

Does your child want to be on the basketball team? Does she strive to be in the class play? Participate in the school concert? It's great news if she does. Kids who get involved in sports, drama, music, or other activities benefit in many ways. Organized activities like these help kids:

- learn teamwork and cooperation
- make new friends who enjoy the same activities
- cope with frustration when they lose
- learn to play fair
- develop empathy for others who miss a basket or fall on the ice
- learn to manage their time so that they can get their homework done, too

For some kids, however, being "the best" can become so important that it overshadows their desire to play or be on the team. Parents are often blamed for emphasizing winning too much. We've all read stories about overenthusiastic parents who stalk the sidelines, argue with coaches, and get ejected from games for arguing balls and strikes. But sometimes the pressure to achieve comes from the kids themselves.

How can you tell if your child is overinvested in winning or in being the star? Here are some signs:

- She gets frustrated and pouts when things don't turn out her way.
- She comes home stressed from the pressure to excel or from competition that's too tough.
- Her life appears to be increasingly unbalanced, so that she has less time for and loses interest in her friends and/or her schoolwork.
- She claims she doesn't want to participate anymore in that sport or activity.
- She feels she is a failure because she didn't get the lead role in the play or score the most points in a game.

If your child has acted in any of these ways, you may have tried to help her see her situation in a larger perspective. If, for example, she didn't get the lead in the play, you might have been tempted to say something like, "You won't remember this ten years from now." That may or may not be true. But the problem with this kind of an answer is that talking about how she'll feel ten years in the future isn't addressing how she feels right now.

You could reassure her that you love her no matter how many goals she scores or what role she plays—that she doesn't have to be the star or the best. That's very important, because she may be craving attention she feels she is missing. Or she may feel that her brother gets more attention or praise than she does because he's better at another activity than she is. Or perhaps she is envious of a classmate who got the solo performance in the school concert because she perceives that this girl is more popular.

But that's still only the first step.

What you can do next is try to help your child just have fun. When nine-year-old Tim didn't win a starting position on his football team because the coach said he was too little, he didn't want to participate at all. Tim's dad first assured Tim that not winning the position wasn't Tim's fault, and then asked, "What else are you good at that you enjoy?"

After this conversation, Tim discovered that he was good at soccer. He also discovered that he actually enjoyed the game—he loved running up and down the field and kicking the ball. And because he felt good about himself on the field, he had an easy time making new friends. He soon came to realize that having fun with his friends was more important than being the star.

Whatever your child does, help him try to do his best. But it's also important to help your child think about the intrinsic rewards in every activity.

## Put an End to Whining

What's more grating than listening to a whining child? Just about as soon as they can talk, kids learn that they can whine when they can't have what they want, or when they don't get it soon enough, or whenever things don't go their way. If it becomes entrenched, the habit is hard to shake.

For many parents, whining is the "fingernails on the blackboard" experience—the behavior that's hardest to bear. It's an infuriating mixture of a certain tone of voice, facial expression, and body posture that is designed to drive parents to distraction.

Every parent is tempted to do anything just to make it stop. You can try ignoring your whining daughter, tell her to stop, beg her to be quiet, or just give in. The problem is that none of these will help her break the whining habit. In fact, giving in may inadvertently let her know that whining will get her what she wants.

Before reacting to this annoying behavior, think about *why* your child is whining. Some children who whine don't want to be pains in the neck. They simply don't know how else to act when they're frustrated. Others do know that whining will annoy you and intentionally set out to do just that.

But regardless of their motivation, they don't fully understand the impact of their behavior on other people. That understanding needs to be expanded in a compassionate way. You can use the problem-solving method to accomplish this; it will help your child think about what she's doing from a new perspective.

First, ask your child, "How do you feel when your sister or brother or a friend whines to you?" This question may take her by surprise. She may never have stopped to consider that one's tone of voice can have an impact on others. For perhaps the first time, she may focus on the effect that whining has on her. She'll probably talk about how much she dislikes it.

That's when you ask, "How do you think I feel when you nag and whine so much?"

At this point, she'll probably be able to realize that if she dislikes it so intensely, you probably do, too.

Then ask, "How do you really feel inside when you whine?"

This question also helps your child address something else she may have never before considered: the fact that she whines because of how she feels inside. Once she's able to identify her feelings, she'll be less at the mercy of them and more in charge of how to express them.

Next ask, "Can you think of a *different* way to let me know how you feel right now?"

This helps her realize that she has options—that there are choices she can make as to how to express herself. By age eight or nine, many children are able to come up with solutions like, "When I feel like whining, I can make myself calm down first and then ask for what I want in a calm voice."

Then ask, "How do you think I'll feel if you do that?" At this point, your child will be able to acknowledge that you will appreciate her calm voice.

Finally, ask, "How will you feel about that?" This question helps your child realize that she'll feel more in control when she's able to master her emotions.

This is not to suggest that children should think that if they don't whine, they'll automatically get what they want. If they want something they truly cannot have, for any reason, they may resort to whining once again. It's important that kids learn to problem-solve in order to get the things that they can have and learn to cope with the frustration that results when they can't have the things they want.

Four-year-old Rafael, for example, wanted a new truck. "I don't want to buy you a new truck," his mother explained, "because you keep pulling the wheels off your old trucks." But Rafael kept whining—"Please, Mom, I really need a new truck. This time I won't break it." At first she was unmoved. But when she saw how frustrated he was becoming, she realized she had to try a new approach.

"What can you do so I will know you will not pull the wheels off?" she asked.

Rafael thought for a moment, then said calmly, "Buy me a little one and I'll show you I won't do it."

Mom agreed. She bought her son an inexpensive small truck and monitored how Rafael played with it. When she saw that he was keeping his word, she regained her trust in him. She then bought him the truck he wanted.

A few years later, Rafael wanted a computer in his room. When his parents said no, he resorted to whining. But he quickly realized that this was a different situation than the one with the truck—his parents couldn't afford to buy a new computer exclusively for him. Instead of whining, he considered ways everyone could share the computer that the family already owned.

It's helpful to keep in mind that whining isn't usually the problem; often, it's the result of the problem.

## Help Kids Learn to Be Resilient

Four-year-old Robert asks Mac for a turn with the truck Mac is playing with. Mac says no. Robert hits him. He knows no other way to get what he wants.

Six-year-old Sarah asks Abbie if she can hold Abbie's doll. Abbie says no, so Sarah just gives up and walks away. She also lacks an alternative idea to achieve her desire.

Eight-year-old Donnie can't complete the jigsaw puzzle he took apart and starts throwing pieces across the room.

How does your child cope with frustration? Does he pout? Walk away? Lash out? Give up too soon? Or does he bounce back and find a different, more effective way to cope with his frustration?

When four-year-old Zachary asked Seth if he could borrow his wagon, Seth refused, explaining that he needed the wagon to pull some rocks. Zach then said, "I'll give it right back." When Seth still refused, Zachary did not lash out or give up. Though he may have thought about hitting Seth or just pulling the wagon away, he didn't—because he also thought about what might happen next if he did that. He realized that Seth might grab the wagon back, they'd fight, and he'd lose a friend. He'd also lose the opportunity to play with the wagon.

So, being a good problem solver, he tried again. Searching for a way to satisfy both himself and Seth so that their needs would mesh instead of conflict, he said, "I'll help you with the rocks!"

This way, Seth could still play with the wagon—while Zachary could play with it, too. This time, Seth agreed, and the two played happily with the wagon together. Zachary's ability to think of another way to solve his problem led to success instead of anger or frustration.

Had their teacher stifled Zachary's way of thinking by demanding that Seth let Zachary have the wagon because he already had his turn, or suggesting that the boys play together or take turns, or, as some teachers and parents might, taking away the wagon so neither boy would have it, Zachary would have been deprived of his opportunity to bounce back the way he did.

While Zachary was successful at getting to play with the wagon at that moment, I do not mean to convey that I believe children should always end up with what they want "now." Mandy, age four, wanted to finger-paint just minutes before her mom needed to set the table for lunch. Her mom explained why she couldn't finger-paint at that time, and then asked, "Can you think of something *different* to do while you wait?"

Mandy thought for a moment (an important step in itself), then gleefully shouted, "I'll read my book." Had her mom simply explained that she needed the table for lunch and then suggested that she "read a book," Mandy might well have whined, "But I want to finger-paint." But like Zachary, she too bounced back. She learned how to wait for what she wants.

In their book *Raising Resilient Children*, Robert Brooks and Sam Goldstein help us understand why some children are more resilient than others; that is, why they are able to overcome obstacles. According to the authors, one way to help children succeed without giving up is to consider other people's points of view. In other words, if we want our children to understand our point of view, we must first show them that we understand theirs. For example, if we yell at our kids who are having trouble with their homework and say, "Try harder," or "Put your mind to it," we are motivated by our own frustration; we're not thinking of how our children will perceive these words. Not surprisingly, most children don't hear comments like these as helpful reminders; they hear judgment and accusation. And they're quick to tune them out—and can you blame them?

---

If we want our children to understand our point of view, we must first show them that we understand theirs.

---

James's parents grew concerned that James wasn't able to persist and complete his homework. They put themselves in his place and considered what words he would like to hear. They began by saying that they appreciated that homework was difficult, and that they were sorry James was having so much trouble with it. When James realized that his parents weren't degrading him, he was ready to think about how he could solve this problem. He enthusiastically created his own plan—to do his hardest homework first, immediately after arriving home, when he had the most energy. Because the plan came from him, he didn't need to be told to try harder or put his mind to it.

Showing our children that we care about them will help them care about themselves. And when we help them think of more than one way to solve a problem, they will tell themselves to try harder and will be less likely to give up.

## "My Kids Wish for What They Don't Have"

We all want things we don't have. Some of us want to be thinner; some of us want to have more hair. Just about everyone wishes for more money. When we make our annual New Year's resolutions, we're reflecting on who we are and who we wish to become.

Kids have many wishes, too. Some want to do better in school, or excel at sports or a hobby, or get along better with a sibling. They want to be taller, or faster, or popular. As frustrated as we feel when we can't achieve the things we want, kids get even more discouraged. Assuring them that some things will come in time often doesn't help, since the future seems so far away to them.

Here's another way to reflect on what we want in our lives, inspired by a book called *If. . . (Questions for the Game of Life)* by Evelyn McFarlane and James Saywell. Though designed primarily for adults, the questions it contains are intended to stimulate anyone's imagination to think about the perfect home, the perfect life, the perfect world. Kids can think about these things, too.

I posed some age-appropriate questions from the book to four boys—twins Allen and Manny, twelve, and eleven-year-olds Lance and Bert. Here are some of their responses.

To the question, "*If* you could be granted one wish, what would it be?" both twins—out of earshot of each other—said, "To live forever."

Lance hoped for "everyone in the world to be happy and live a nice life." Bert wished for peace.

I then asked, "*If* you could become famous for something you don't currently do, what would it be?"

Allen dreamed of being in the movies. Manny said he would become a basketball player. Lance and Bert both wished to be famous baseball players. When I asked what they would do *if* they could become invisible, Lance said that he'd "sneak into a baseball game, go onto the field and into the dugout, and listen to what they say." Consistent with his wish for peace, Bert would "go to the White House while they were having a meeting and listen to what they were saying about war."

Next, I asked a question rooted in the real world: *If* they could change one personality trait, which one would it be? Allen said he'd stop procrastinating with his schoolwork. Manny, Bert, and Lance all recognized the need to not lose control when someone makes them mad. I then asked each boy how he might go about changing these things. Allen said, "That's hard because I like to play on my computer and before I know it, it's time to go to bed." Then he paused, smiled, and said softly, "I guess I should do my homework first."

Allen and Manny acknowledged that their sister "bugs" them "all the time": "like when I have friends over," said Allen; and "when I'm playing my video games," said Manny. Allen thought that closing his door so his sister couldn't get in would help keep her out, and Manny considered playing his games when his sister wasn't home. Lance, who "loses it" when his mom won't let him watch TV after dinner, also realized upon reflection, "Maybe I should do my homework first."

Interestingly, when asked what else they would change about themselves *if* they could, all the boys wished they could be taller. Why? Allen said he could "lunge farther." Manny could "reach for higher things and jump higher," and Lance thought he'd "fit in more with other kids."

I then asked the boys another important question of my own: "What's good about being short?"

Allen paused and then said, "You're unique."

Manny thought and said, "I have more agility. And I can fit through things. And it helps me be a good squash player; I can get lower to the ground."

Lance smiled and whispered, "And I can fit into smaller places."

Making positives out of negatives, as Lance did, can stop us from dwelling on what we can't have or our dissatisfaction with what we do have. Joshua, who is eight and wishes he were taller, told me that he keeps looking at his friends who are taller and wishing he could be like them. He had to think really hard about what's good about being short, but I encouraged him and he finally said, "When I'm bullied and a kid won't give my ball back, I can crawl under his legs and get it." He then added, "When I play football, all the kids are tall and they won't tackle me because they look right over me and don't see me." He laughed after he said this, confessing that he was "just kidding"—but what struck me is that this may have been the first time in his life Joshua laughed about being too short.

When kids play the "if" game, they not only have fun fantasizing but also end up feeling better about the things they can't change. The game also allows them to identify what they can change and resolve to make those changes. Some things can become more than just a wish—*if* we work hard to make them come true.

# 3

# Stress, Worries, Fears, and Trauma

## Starting School or a New School

Your child is going to school for the first time. If you've moved, perhaps she's starting a new school. Or maybe she's moving up from elementary to middle school. The good news is that most children adjust quite quickly and take the transition in stride. Others have more trouble making the change. If your child particularly liked her old school, or enjoyed her routine at home, her transition may prove slower or more difficult than you anticipated.

It's important to keep in mind that there's no single timetable for making transitions: how well we adapt to change is a matter of temperament. Also, remember that a child doesn't have the same broad perspective that adults do: to them, starting school for the first time or changing schools means that their whole world is changing.

But getting children off to a good start in a new school couldn't be more important. According to Lynn Huffman and her colleagues, in a new report issued by the Child Mental Health Foundations and Agencies Network, children who enter kindergarten unhappy, fearful, or angry are too preoccupied to form good relationships with teachers and classmates. Thus, they're unable to participate fully in the experience of learning.

Here's how you can help keep transition stress to a minimum.

- If possible, visit the school with your child to meet the teacher and staff before the first day.

- Tell your child a story about a time you moved or began a new school. Kids like to hear about when we were their age.
- Go to the store and let her pick out some school supplies, like notebooks and a lunch box. Encourage her to also find something special—maybe a fancy pencil case. That way, these materials are hers.
- Plan on walking her to school or to the bus stop on the first day if at all possible.
- Help her problem-solve ways to make new friends, and to stay in touch with old friends.
- Since you are the one constant in your child's life right now, it's important to listen to your child's thoughts and feelings. Encourage her to ask questions and ask some questions yourself. Start with the positive.

One dad I know took his daughter Jodi, age five, to the store to buy school supplies. On the way there, he began asking her some questions:

**Dad:** Jodi, you're going to kindergarten soon. Tell me what you think you'll like about school.
**Jodi:** The toys.
**Dad:** And what else do you think you'll like?
**Jodi:** My teacher.
**Dad:** Good thinking. You thought of two things you'll like about school. Can you think of something else you'll like?
**Jodi:** Uh, I don't know.
**Dad:** I bet if you think really hard you can think of one more thing.
**Jodi:** Yeah . . . and I can paint and play with kids in the playground.

It's also important to listen to all your child's feelings. However excited she might be about beginning a new school, she can also be feeling anxious. Often we have mixed emotions about things—we're looking forward to something, but it also makes us nervous. We think one should cancel the other out when in truth they both exist side by side.

These mixed emotions are part of life, but they're very hard to talk about. Here's how you can help a five-year-old express and cope with good and not-so-good feelings:

**Dad:** You thought of things that you will like about going to school. Is there anything that might not make you happy?

**Jodi:** I might not have a friend.

**Dad:** Can you think of one thing you can do to find a new friend?

**Jodi:** Share my new doll.

**Dad:** Good thinking. You're a good problem solver.

Helping your child acknowledge both sets of feelings helps them manage their difficult feelings. If you talk with your child ahead of time about her full range of feelings, she'll be better prepared to handle a new school experience.

## Test Stress: What You Can Do

Is your child afraid of school tests? Some kids are, even as early as age five or six. If you see a fearful pattern beginning to emerge, you will probably want to ask your child why he's afraid. But most likely you'll hear the perennial, "I don't know."

Stay calm. If you're upset about his anxiety, your child will sense it. But don't dismiss his fear, either, by saying, "You'll do fine." Your child will sense a distinct lack of caring about his feelings. It's also important to avoid showing disappointment in a bad grade. Instead of telling your child how you feel about the grade, let your child express how he feels about it.

What you need to do next is determine why he's afraid and what exactly the problem is. Test anxiety can have several different causes, and you can often find the source of the problem if you go over the test with your child.

Some children don't do well on tests and come to fear them. If this is the case, you can try coaching your child in some specific test-taking strategies, such as those described by Joseph Casbarro in his book *Test Anxiety and What You Can Do About It*. These include looking over the entire test before starting, eliminating choices in a multiple-choice exam that your child knows for sure are incorrect, answering easy items first, and watching the time.

Another possibility is that your child knew the answers and still failed a test, which makes him afraid to try again. Try to determine if your child read the questions too quickly or failed  to understand the directions. Many kids misread directions and questions, often from carelessness. If this is the case with your child, have him practice reading more slowly and carefully.

Some children fear tests even when they don't fail. It may be that your child is afraid of making mistakes. If so, let him know that everybody does. Another possibility is that your child may worry about letting you down. He may feel that too much emphasis is placed on achievement or that he receives praise only when he does well. One parent I know criticized her daughter for getting a 98 on a math test. Instead of focusing on the positive score, she questioned her child about what she got wrong.

But the problem may run deeper. Your child may be distracted because she's overscheduled and has too much to do. Many kids these days are trying to do too much, too soon, too fast—music lessons, dance classes, soccer practice, Girl Scouts—all in addition to getting their homework done on time. How much can your child take? How much can *you* take?

The ancient Greeks had a very important belief: "Everything in moderation." This applies to children, too. With your help, children as young as seven can plan their own days. Here's how you can help:

- Make a list of all the activities your child participates in—and any new ones she has expressed interest in.
- Ask your child to cross out anything she would or could discontinue.
- Of the remaining activities, ask her to put a star next to those that she must have in her life.
- Let your child plan her time. Include time for homework and that important time to just play with her friends.
- Ask her if she thinks there's time for all the activities in her plan.

After going through this process, most children will see the need to make important choices in life, such as how to decide which activities are of greatest interest to them. If your daughter thinks a different activity once a week for an hour is enough to satisfy her, let her try that. If your son would rather spend time perfecting skills in one area, that's OK, too. What's important is that they made the decision themselves: kids will learn to schedule time for what they have to do and still have time for what they want to do. They are more likely to stick to their own plan—altering it when necessary to better suit their needs—than one their parents created.

Balance, moderation, and a plan of their own will help your children feel more in control, better prepared for their tests, and less stressed. And the less stress they're under, the less you'll be under as well.

---

Kids will learn to schedule time for what they have to do and still have time for what they want to do.

---

As Maurice Elias of Rutgers University tells us, "We must prepare our children for the tests of life, not a life of tests." And by doing that, they may actually feel less anxious about the tests they have to take.

## Less Stress Means More Learning

Toni, eleven, had been a good student all through elementary school. But when she began sixth grade in middle school, her grades began falling—especially in math, which was odd, since that had always been her best subject and the one she most enjoyed. Also uncharacteristically, she began complaining that she couldn't fall asleep at night and that she was plagued by vague stomach pains and headaches. She began biting her nails—something she'd never done. Toni was suffering from stress.

How does generalized emotional stress affect how kids learn? Gene Carter, executive director of the Association for Supervision and Curriculum Development, a national educational organization, thinks many kids have problems in school for emotional reasons. He believes that students cannot devote their full attention to learning when they feel stressed or powerless. My own research backs this up: youngsters who are able to make good decisions in their lives are more likely to succeed with other people. They feel less anxiety and can devote more attention to learning.

Kids who cannot solve everyday social problems that arise with classmates, siblings, teachers, or parents may become frustrated and angry. Failure after failure may cause children to lash out or do the opposite—to give up too soon and even withdraw from people and problems they cannot solve. On the other hand, children who are able to communicate easily with others at school are better able to give their full attention to the process of learning. They can listen, pay attention, and persist at challenging tasks.

You can help your child learn to talk about his thoughts and feelings by asking questions such as:

"What happened in school today that made you feel happy?"
"Did anything happen that made you feel sad?"
"Did you do or say anything to help yourself feel better?"

Any emotional stress that may prevent children from concentrating on their schoolwork can cause them to become anxious about school. But children can learn skills to solve the emotional problems that are blocking them. When I spoke to Toni, for example, I asked her what had happened in school to make her feel sad. She explained to me that the other kids were tormenting her about being too skinny and having an ugly birthmark on her face. One of the worst offenders was in her math class. "I can't concentrate on my work when kids make me feel so bad," she told me.

When I asked her what she could do to solve this problem, she thought hard about this. She decided that when it was her turn to read her book report to the class, she would add a story about a fictional girl who was called too skinny and ugly. In her story, she explained how the fictional girl felt about what her classmates were doing. In this way, she didn't give up but rather took control. The kids who treated her this way connected her story with what they were doing and began to see her in a new light. In time, she even made friends with some of the kids who taunted her. With this problem solved, she felt free to concentrate on her work.

Perhaps solving "people" problems is just as important as solving problems in math. Kids who are afraid to go to school, are teased, or can't make the friends they so desperately crave are too preoccupied to think about the tasks at hand. If we can appreciate that kids who fail in math may not necessarily need more math, we may go a long way in helping them focus and facilitate their learning.

## Too Shy to Participate?

Does your child choose not to play with others or seem fearful of joining in a group, preferring to watch others rather than participate himself? Is she too afraid to stand up in front of her class and read her book report or raise her hand to answer a question the teacher asks?

Many children may feel stress and temporarily withdraw from activities and from peers in a new situation, such as attending a different school, but as soon as they gain a sense of confidence, they become engaged and active. But some children are so shy, timid, or fearful of others that they are unable to assert themselves or stand up for their rights, and if they are denied a request, may pout and give up—too soon. And although waiting for what we want is an important skill in life, shy and withdrawn children may wait too long—because they cannot or choose not to try again. These children need help overcoming their fears.

Richie, ten, was too frightened to participate in class. He believed that if he made a mistake, the kids would laugh at him or the teacher would compare him to kids who knew the answers. His mom pleaded with him to try; and telling him, even promising him, that the kids wouldn't laugh and the teacher wouldn't make him feel bad didn't change his beliefs. Finally, she offered to buy him that new puppy he'd been begging for, if only he would speak up in class. But a new puppy would not solve the real problem—why he was so anxious in school.

Here are some things you can do if your child feels the way Richie did. Ask such questions as:

"Is it something your teacher does?"
"Are you worried you might make a mistake?"
"Are you embarrassed to be called on?"
"Do kids tease you when you talk out loud?"

Once your child has identified the causes of his discomfort, ask him how he feels when the teacher calls on him, and acknowledge those feelings. Then:

- If others tease or laugh at him when he answers a question in class, ask him to tell you what he can do or say to get them to stop.
- If he fears making mistakes, let him know it's OK to make them. Tell him about some that you make, or some you made when you were his age.
- Ask him if he can try answering just one question. Let him pick the subject, and talk to him about waiting until he hears a question he's sure about.
- If he has to read aloud, let him practice that at home, in an environment he perceives as safe, with you there to support him.

Jesse, seven, had anxieties of a different kind. He was timid about joining in play with others, because in the past, kids he asked to play said things like, "Not now," or "We don't have room for any more kids in here." Jesse had given up and, like many shy and anxious children, felt sad. Jesse's mom engaged her son in a technique found to be helpful by clinicians: role-playing. Pretending to be a child, Mom asked her son to show her how he asks others to play. "Hi, can I play?" responded Jesse. Mom noticed that his head was down and he spoke so softly she could hardly hear him. Mom then said, "That was good. But this time, look at me and speak a little louder so I can hear you." After Jesse practiced this for a while, Mom brought in his slightly older sister so he could practice with her.

Teaching children social skills such as eye contact and speaking up is one way to help. Another way is to ask questions that help children think of concrete strategies if one way does not work. Four-year-old Tanya wanted to play in the doll corner at preschool; when the kids didn't invite her in, she just hovered around the doll corner, not knowing how to convey that she wanted to join in. Meaning well, her teacher offered, "Tanya would like to help pack the suitcase." But even if the kids had welcomed her, Tanya was not ready. And her teacher was thinking for her.

Tanya's mom said, "I have a problem for you to solve. Try to think of three ways to get 'Allie the Alligator' [her favorite puppet] to go swimming with you." Her ideas were not evaluated because she wanted to free Tanya to think of more than one way to solve this problem. Tanya enjoyed thinking of ways to entice Allie to swim with her, especially her idea that she gleefully shouted, "Tell him I'll save him if he drowns." One day, soon after, Tanya was standing outside that same doll corner in school and informed them, "If you need a firefighter, I'm a firefighter." Just then, one of the kids happened to spot a pretend fire.

Tanya was so excited that she came home beaming and proudly proclaimed, "Mommy, I solved a problem today!"

Heather's mom was bewildered that her seven-year-old consistently retreated to her room whenever she had company, even when her guests brought their children for Heather to play with. Mom tried luring her by telling her how much people wanted to see her, explaining that there would be presents for her, and pleading with her to join in. Nothing changed Heather's mind. She was simply too shy to greet the company.

Last Christmas, Heather's mom tried something unique. She told Heather, "I am making a gingerbread man for the holidays, and I need your help." When it was time to make the face, Mom said, "You can put the eyes and nose and mouth anyplace you want. Be silly. Have fun." With sugar, Heather shaped the mouth and put it on the gingerbread man's forehead. She used candy balls and placed them under his mouth. She put his nose, made out of licorice, under the right eye. Heather laughed so loud she could hardly stop. She was so excited to show off her new creation that she couldn't wait for the company to come. When they did arrive, instead of running to her room, Heather ran to the guests as each entered the house and led them to her work of art. By the next party, Heather had already decided to create designs for cookies and write her own poem for each guest. Her mom doesn't have to lure her with promises of presents, explain how much people want to see her, or plead with her anymore.

If you have a child who is too shy to participate, help your child feel relaxed and calm. If she can feel proud of her book report, confident about new ways to join others in play, or excited about her creations for guests who visit, she will go a long way toward feeling free of her fears and trepidation and safe to join in instead of retreating.

## When a Family Member Is Chronically Ill

When you, your spouse, or one of your children comes down with a bad cold or the flu, you often feel frustrated, anxious, even angry that this had to happen now. Everything moves more slowly and even the simplest task can become enormously complicated. Normal routines are interrupted.

What must it feel like when a family member has a lifelong physical disability or a life-threatening illness? The anxiety, strain, and even depression can become overwhelming and seemingly impossible to endure.

Montel Williams, a well-known syndicated talk-show host, was diagnosed with multiple sclerosis (MS), a potentially life-threatening inflammatory disease of the central nervous system. Montel does not allow himself to succumb to despair or walk around in a state of shock, however. Recognizing the link between physical fitness and health, Montel embarked upon a course of physical fitness activity to look good and to feel as good as he looked. He felt he owed it not only to himself but to his children, aged nine, ten, fourteen, and nineteen.

I had the opportunity to talk with Montel about physical fitness. For him, it's about how feeling good physically has helped him feel good emotionally, and it's given him more energy to be with and play with his children. "Once you start thinking about your own physical health and well-being," he explained, "it opens you up to be more concerned about the people you love—your spouse, your kids." He feels that his inner strength—enhanced through exercises he and his fitness trainer, Wini Linguvic, describe in their book, *Body Change*—has had a powerful effect on his family.

Believing it's important to be totally honest, Montel fully explained his illness to his kids, including how MS can lead to progressive degeneration. He also expressed his need for uninterrupted time in the gym for one hour each morning.

Montel understood that explaining his illness and his needs to his children would help them become more empathic not only to him but to the needs and feelings of others as well—such as kids who are bullied at school. Montel shared with me stories about how his kids now want to help people who are in wheelchairs, or who walk slowly in the mall, or who seem sad. "They understand that even though I look healthy now, I have this illness, and they are well prepared for any changes in the future," Montel said.

Just as his kids have become more sensitive to others because of their dad's illness, Montel believes he's become more sensitive to his kids. "It makes me more aware of their needs than I might otherwise have been," he said.

Montel couldn't predict how long he'll look and feel as good as he does right now. In the meantime, he's living his life to the fullest and—with the help of his fitness trainer—doing everything he can while he is able.

Brandy Haller, now five, was diagnosed at age two with pulmonary hypertension, a rare, potentially fatal lung disease that is often mistaken for asthma or shortness of breath. For the past three years, Brandy has had to wear a tube that pumps blood and lifesaving medicines into her heart twenty-four hours a day, seven days a week. While she doesn't understand the seriousness of her disease, she does understand that her pump cannot get wet or be pulled out, and because of that she can't go to the beach and play in the sand and water. But with her "pumpy," as she calls it, Brandy remains cheerful, rides her bike, and doesn't complain.

While her mom and dad hope every day for a cure, they remain upbeat yet realistic in their day-to-day lives. As Brandy's mom explained, "We have a greater appreciation of every day. We can't think about tomorrow or five years from now or what she wants to be when she grows up. We have to look at the positive and have as much fun as we can now."

Brandy is now in kindergarten. Although her teachers are well informed of her condition and special needs and what to do in case of an emergency, Brandy's mom and dad know that sending her to school is a risk. But they are determined to remain positive. "Brandy loves people," her mom told me. "I want her to enjoy them, and we'll deal with problems as they come up."

Families like these who cope so well can inspire us all. When we feel stressed or overwhelmed, thinking about Montel, his family, and the Hallers can help to pull us through. If they can stay positive and see that life is worth living, so can we.

# Coping with Loss

## Rethinking Divorce: It Doesn't Always Have to Hurt Your Child

Do children living with unhappily married parents fare better than children living with a divorced parent? For years, we have been advised that children of divorce, especially boys, lose interest in their friends, do poorly in school, and are likely to grow up with severe emotional scars.

Parents can rest easier now.

E. Mavis Hetherington studied twenty-five hundred children from fourteen hundred families for close to thirty years to see how they adjusted to divorce (her findings appear in *For Better or for Worse*, written with John Kelly). She found that 75–80 percent of children of divorce have established careers, are enjoying meaningful relationships, and are successful in life—whether or not their parents remarried. While 10 percent of youngsters from nondivorced families experienced troubled adulthood, most came from families where conflict was frequent. However, those from divorced and nondivorced families experiencing high conflict were somewhat more likely themselves to divorce (36 percent from divorced, 29 percent from intact high-conflict families) than those from low-conflict nondivorced families (18 percent). Hetherington does point out, however, that children of divorce are more likely to succeed in their own marriages if their spouses are from low-conflict nondivorced families because those spouses are better able than ones who experienced divorce to be supportive of the emotional needs of their partners.

Hetherington acknowledges that divorce is initially very painful for almost all families, even when one or both spouses feel less stressed afterward. Despite new emotional and financial strain, she believes that how youngsters turn out depends on the extent to which the parents take hold of their own lives and on how sensitive and supportive they are to their children's needs. Jill, mother of twins Ethan and Bob, who divorced their father when the boys were only three, tried very hard to think of her children's needs as well as her own. She respected her children's feelings right from the start.

For example, when Ethan asked, "Why doesn't Daddy live here anymore?" Jill answered—simply and honestly—"Because we don't get along."

When the twins were ten, their father lost his job and he could no longer afford to support the boys' participation in a hockey league. Jill knew how much hockey meant to them, so she took on an extra job to defray the cost. Without berating their father, she found a way to respect her sons' needs.

Throughout the boys' formative years, both their father and Jill followed consistent rules, offered by Hetherington and other experts:

- Be honest.
- Let your children know you love them and will take care of them.
- Assure them that what happened is not their fault.
- Avoid blaming or criticizing the other parent.
- Let the noncustodial parent visit and participate in your children's lives in a consistent way.
- Let your children express their thoughts and feelings—and *listen* when they do. Assure them that you understand.
- Respect your children's needs.
- Communicate with your ex-spouse—so that you can be consistent about rules and discipline and so that you don't buy the same gifts at birthdays and holidays.
- Respect your ex-spouse; don't get involved in "one-upping" him or her.
- Be aware of those times when your child tries to play one parent against the other. If you think that is happening, talk to your child

about it. Ask her to think about how you feel. Ask her to think about how she really feels, too.

No matter how well you handle divorce, certain times of the year feel extra challenging, like the holiday season and birthdays. These are times when expectations run high, and everyone has memories of spending time together. It's especially important for divorced parents to cooperate in terms of time, logistics, and presents.

Today, Ethan and Bob are college juniors. They hold responsible jobs to help pay for their tuition, have good friends, and get along well with both parents. When their mother remarried, they were happy and supportive.

Perhaps these boys learned to care about others because others cared about them.

## When a Best Friend Moves Away

A friend is someone we do things with, care about, and trust. We tell them our troubles, and they make us feel better. They're there when we need them, and we're there for them. What happens when we learn that someone has to move and we're going to be separated?

When the Gladwell family learned that their friends, the Morans, had to relocate, the news was devastating. Not only were their daughters the same ages, but the moms had also become best friends. "I know they're only moving an hour away," explained Martha Gladwell, "but it just won't be the same. Now we do things on the spur of the moment, like go to the movies or just make popcorn. After they move, everything will have to be planned. I feel the loss for myself as much as I do for my kids. I didn't even realize how intertwined our lives had become until I learned they were leaving."

Martha had other feelings that were harder to express: that her friends were moving on with their lives while she was being left behind. Then she added, "But I have to be strong. I don't want my kids to see me crying."

When Martha asked her children what they would miss most after their friends moved, Kris, twelve, the oldest, lamented, "riding to school together on the bus," and "just being able to walk over and say hello."

Micki, age eleven, said she would miss her friend "just being there." Martha talked to her daughters about the importance of accepting those feelings. She went out of her way to *not* say things like, "In time you won't feel so sad." As Martha explained, "It's not true; I don't know how they'll feel in time. And a statement like that certainly won't help them get through the painful feelings they're facing right now."

One thing Martha planned on doing was making dates for the families to get together on a regular basis, for both formal occasions, like holidays and birthdays, and informal get-togethers, like meeting at the mall. If the distance separating the friends isn't too far to make visits prohibitive, this is one of the most helpful things you can do.

Yet another way to help children sort through their feelings about lost friendships is to read books on the subject. In *Amber Brown Goes Fourth*, author Paula Danziger relates the story of a fourth-grader, Amber Brown, whose best friend, Justin, moved away. Humorous yet insightful, the book describes how Amber was at first so preoccupied with missing Justin that she didn't even notice that another classmate, Brandi, needed a new friend as much as she did and had been interested in becoming friends with her all along. Slowly, Amber opens herself up to the new friendship while learning an important lesson: even though Brandi isn't Justin, Amber and Brandi could still be new best friends.

Eight-year-old Kira, whose friend moved to a different neighborhood, loves this story. Even though her friend would still be close by, she felt the pain nonetheless. "She's not in my school," she explained, "and we can't play together at recess." Kira's mom, Margaret, helped her think of her own ideas for coping with this important change in her life. First, she asked Kira how friends could stay connected if they lived far away from each other.

"They could call each other on the phone, send e-mails, and instant-message them, or get together for a special vacation somewhere," Kira suggested. Kira's friend, who was visiting during this discussion, had one more idea, "Send pictures to each other, so they can see what they look like as they get older." Then Margaret asked her daughter how she could stay in touch with her own friend. After thinking about this for a while, Kira came up with some ideas: "Make playdates together," and "Go places together."

While friendships may become less intense with physical distance, and in many cases completely disappear in time, keeping in touch, at least at first, may soften the blow. It also helps to remember something that Martha realized a few weeks after the Morans had left: "It's hard getting used to the loss, but maybe this is a good way to prepare my daughters for more permanent losses, such as when their grandparents die. Maybe undergoing this experience will help my girls learn to appreciate what we have while we have it. I know it's had that effect on me."

That's an important message for all of us. When life surprises us with situations we didn't anticipate, we can use these experiences as stepping-stones to the future, as opportunities to grow and adapt. We can never be sure of what will happen next, but we can have confidence in our ability to problem-solve.

## Helping Your Child Cope with the Death of a Loved One

Death is a natural part of life. While we may want to shield our children from the experience of loss, we can't. And we would be doing them a disservice if we did. Understanding what it means to lose a loved one is part of what it means to be human.

At the same time, we have to acknowledge that a child's conception of death and loss differs significantly from ours, and that it evolves as children grow.

"In the midst of the confusion and pain when death occurs, adult caregivers may be at a loss as to how to best give their children the care and support they need," says Janis Keyser, codirector of the Center for Grieving Children, Teens, and Families in Philadelphia, Pennsylvania.* She adds that although very young children might not understand the words *died* and *dead* right now, it is important to use them and not substitute for those words to avoid the truth or to buffer sadness. As she explained, "Children

---

*The center provides support groups for grieving families with children of all ages, as well as workshops for professionals who work with them. For more information, go to www. grievingchildren.org, e-mail the center at grievingchildren@aol.com, or call 215-427-6767.

tend to be very literal. If you euphemistically tell your preschooler that 'We lost Grandpa,' you may well find your child looking in the closet for him."

Equally unhelpful are statements like, "God took Daddy," or "Daddy's sleeping with God." Very young children can become fearful of God or afraid to go to sleep. Other comments to avoid, Keyser advises, are, "Daddy got sick," because next time the young child gets a head cold, he might become fearful of dying, too. If Dad died from an illness, it's better to explain that "Daddy was very, very sick, and the doctors couldn't help."

Here's how one mom prepared Lindsay, her eight-year-old daughter, for the death of her grandmother, who had terminal cancer. "I have good news and bad news," she told Lindsay. "The good news is that Grandma won't have to have any more operations because they won't help her—and you know how much pain she used to be in after the operations. The bad news is that the germs may be getting stronger. The doctors are going to try a new medicine, but we don't know if that will work."

When Lindsay asked if Grandma could come to her soccer games, her mom explained that Grandma can't do many of the things she used to be able to do—"Grandma is very, very sick and she's very, very tired." When Lindsay changed the subject, her mom stopped talking about it. "As a rule, I only talk about her grandmother for as long as Lindsay's interested," her mom explained. "And when we do talk about it, I don't tell her directly that Grandma is dying—but if she asked, I wouldn't lie. I would tell her that Grandma may die, but no one knows when."

There are also many ways to ease the sting of death by helping your child realize that your loved one lives on. Here are some other tips offered by Keyser and her codirector, Rob Sheesley:

- Learn how your children can best describe their feelings. Some may be more comfortable drawing or writing a poem, while others may want to act out moments of joy they remember with their loved one.
- Share your own feelings with your children. If they ask such questions as, "Why isn't Daddy coming home?" you can say things like, "I miss Daddy, too."
- Answer questions they ask, not questions they do not. Answer briefly, but honestly.

- Talk about rituals. Remembering things you did as a family on the birthday of the person who died or on holidays will help your loved one live on.
- Include the person in everyday conversation. When I'm with a friend and we arrive someplace so early that we have to wait, I say, "As my dad always said, 'It's better to be thirty minutes early than one minute late.'" In this way, my dad remains very much a presence in my life.
- Read books about how death is a part of life. For example, books for four- to eight-year-olds that explain death in non-anxiety-producing ways include *Lifetimes: The Beautiful Way to Explain Death to Children* by Bryan Mellonie and Robert Ingpen, and *When Dinosaurs Die* by Laurie Krasny and Marc Brown.

In addition to these tips, try to seek support for the whole family. Though your priority may be to help your child through the grieving process, you are simultaneously experiencing your own grief and loss. Joining a support group is one way to find your own inner strength. These groups, says Keyser, "can help create a sense of safety and normalcy for families going through the bereavement process."

## Celebrating Mother's and Father's Days—When Mom or Dad Isn't Here

For children who have a parent who has died, Mother's and Father's Days can be difficult holidays to get through. The first of these holidays that occurs after the death can be particularly hard.

There's no ignoring the situation: the holidays figure prominently in our society and escaping them isn't really an option. Instead, the best plan is to help your children learn about ways to celebrate their deceased parents in their hearts.

"It's very tough for kids to experience the death of a parent," says Lynne Hughes, executive director and founder of Comfort Zone Camp,* a

---

*For more information about Comfort Zone Camp in Rockville, Virginia, designed to help grieving children aged seven through seventeen, call toll-free 866-488-5679, e-mail comfortzonecamp@aol.com, or go to www.comfortzonecamp.org. The camp is free, and travel stipends are available.

national bereavement camp for children, "and if we can find a way to help them maintain connectedness to their loved one, Mother's and Father's Days can be easier for them." Hughes, who lost both parents before the age of twelve, knows the importance of helping kids cope and the value of staying connected. Here are some ideas she shared with me:

- Find ways to commemorate Mom or Dad, tell good stories, and remember good times together.
- Encourage your children to talk about their feelings and share your feelings, too. Let them draw pictures using colors to depict their feelings, such as yellow for happy, blue for sad, and red for angry.
- Create family traditions such as going to Dad's favorite restaurant or Mom's favorite picnic spot, places where the deceased parent's presence is especially strong.
- Create and decorate a "coping box"—your child can use an old shoebox, for example. Suggest that children write down things they can do on days when they especially miss their parent (e-mail a friend, write in a memory book, eat an ice-cream cone), and place these suggestions in the box for future reference.
- When possible, engage a stepparent, grandparent, aunt or uncle, or close family friend to step in and participate in activities earmarked for "father/mother and child" and activities your children remember having done with the deceased parent.

Families at the Comfort Zone Camp have found other creative ways to help their kids cope. One mom took her kids to the zoo on Father's Day because that's where they spent their last Father's Day together. A dad engaged his kids on Mother's Day by having them create a time capsule dedicated to their mom: they collected photographs and mementos, placed them in a special box, and buried them near their mom's favorite tree. In other families, children wrote messages to their dead parents on helium balloons and released them into the air.

"It doesn't really matter what you do," says Hughes. "What really matters is that you do *something*. You can't camouflage the holiday and hope that it will go away. It won't."

It's also important to be proactive. Many teachers, particularly in the younger grades, devote class time to making projects for Mom or Dad in advance of the holiday. If your spouse is deceased, you may want to remind the teacher of your child's situation and encourage him or her to let the children know that they can make a gift in memory of their parent. You can also talk with your child about how she will feel to hear other kids talking about their moms or dads and what she can say about hers.

Jimmy, age ten, reacted on Mother's Day to the loss of his mother two years earlier in a different way. He came home from school appearing quiet and withdrawn. When his stepmother asked what was wrong, Jimmy didn't want to talk about it. "Nothing," he said. But his stepmom was still concerned; she sensed that his feelings of loss may have been heightened by the approaching holiday, so she calmly asked again. This time, Jimmy admitted, "I miss my mom."

Some women might have responded with resentment or envy. But Jimmy's stepmother put her own feelings aside and tried to help him understand the true meaning of the holiday. "What made your mother special to you?" she asked.

Jimmy thought for a moment and said, "It's because of her I was born. And she loved me and listened to me and did things with me."

"Giving birth is important," Jimmy's stepmom replied. "But what really counts is you now. Even though I didn't bring you into the world, do you think I care about you and want to listen to and do things with you?" Jimmy had never thought about this before—that his stepmother could have feelings about him in this way and about celebrating Mother's Day. He came to appreciate that maybe he and his stepmom could find a way to enjoy Mother's Day together.

## When the Family Pet Dies

They sleep in our beds, eat at our tables, rest on our couches, and nestle in our laps. Whether your household includes a dog, cat, bird, or gerbil, pets often become so beloved that we can't imagine family life without them. Having pets teaches children many important lessons about life, and among the most important of these may be learning to cope with issues of illness, old age, and death.

Many parents find that having a pet gives them the perfect opening to talk about some of life's most important and difficult lessons: that all living things die someday, that dying is part of life, and that we have to love and care for one another—our pets included—while they are alive.

Older children can understand that pets don't live as long as we do. In fact, the first day a pet comes into your home may be a great opportunity to talk to older children about natural life spans, how different animals have different life expectancies, and approximately how long this pet may be expected to live.

But what about younger children? What do they understand?

Four-year-old Carl's mother explained to him that it was an accident when Rocky, their puppy, got run over by a car. She said, "We loved Rocky very much. We feel very sad that he died. We'll get another puppy right away."

Carl's mom was trying to comfort her son, believing that the best way to get her son's mind off the pet who died was to replace it with another. But Carl, like many children his age, might have interpreted what his mom told him in quite a different way.

Researchers Annemarie Roeper and Irv Sigel report that some preschoolers are unable to distinguish which living things in their household are and are not part of the family. If Carl thought of Rocky as part of his family, he might have thought, "If I get run over, would Mom get a new boy and forget about me?"

To determine how much he really understands about a pet's death, talk to your child. Ask him, for example:

"What do you think happened when Rocky got run over by a car?"
"How do you feel about this?"

One four-year-old, when asked what he thought had happened to his dog, simply said, "He went to heaven." To this child, heaven is "up in the sky" where people and pets go when they die. He knew the dog was no longer in pain.

When asked how he felt, he said, "Very, very sad." His mom told him that she understood, that she felt sad, too, and that everyone needs time to just feel sad. Talk about the dead pet if your child wants to—but don't force or prolong the conversation if your child changes the subject.

Questions and conversations like these will help you decipher your child's understanding of the permanence of death, whether he understands your concern for his feelings, and whether getting another pet would help.

How can you tell if your child is ready for a new pet? Suggest that you visit an animal shelter together, and then watch carefully to see how he reacts. If he's immediately drawn to a puppy with big ears, then he may be ready for a new pet. If he just stands at the cage and cries, then he's probably not ready yet.

Wait a month or so, and then try again. Eventually, most children are ready to adopt a new animal friend. If you wait until he's really ready, then the new pet won't be a replacement, but a brand-new member of the family, unique in itself. When getting a new pet is your child's idea, he will be less likely to believe that you will forget about the old one easily.

# 5

# Caring and Empathy

## Are We Sending Different Messages
## to Boys and to Girls?

We send our sons and daughters off to school hoping that they will all find an exciting environment for learning, but what actually happens in classrooms across the country is often surprising and disturbing. Here are some research findings I recently discovered:

- By age two, girls are interrupted when they're speaking more than boys are.
- In kindergarten, boys get more attention than girls.
- As early as first grade, teachers call on boys more than girls, and allow them to speak more in class.
- Elementary-school teachers praise girls for how they dress and wear their hair, whereas boys are coached and praised for how they solve problems and accomplish tasks.
- Boys are asked more thought-provoking questions, suggesting that teachers believe boys are more capable of abstract thinking than are girls.
- From preschool through high school, boys receive more of teachers' attention and are given more time to talk.

After summarizing these and other studies on school and gender, researchers Janice Koch, Eli Newberger, Diane Ruble, and Carol Lynn Martin suggest that parents and teachers—without even being aware of it—may be sending different messages to boys and to girls.

Are teachers, however unwittingly, sending a subtle message that boys have more important things to say than girls do?

This kind of inequity doesn't just show up at school, but also at home. Both mothers and fathers encourage boys' gross motor activities more than girls', and allow boys more freedom from adult supervision. Girls receive more encouragement to show dependency and tender emotions. As early as three to six months, mothers smile more at their daughters than at their sons, and at school, day-care staff also smile more at girls than at boys.

Fathers give their sons more commands and demands by saying things like, "Bring me that book." To girls, dads are more likely to say, "Could you please bring me that book?" Not only do parents talk more politely to their girls, but by eighteen months of age, they also include in their conversations with their daughters a greater variety of words conveying emotion—both positive, such as happiness and pride, and negative, primarily sadness and fear—than they do in conversation with their sons.

When parents do talk to their sons about feelings, it is mostly about anger. And when guiding their child through conflict, mothers favor establishing harmony with their daughters but accept retaliation as a solution by their sons. Also, both parents punish children differently: while boys are more likely to be punished for hitting their brother or sister, or for grabbing toys, parents are more likely to explain to girls why they shouldn't do those things.

It seems as if we concentrate on feelings with our daughters and actions with our sons. But this isn't fair to anyone. Girls are interested in doing things even though they may not say so.

Similarly, we encourage our daughters to experience their emotions and expect our sons to control theirs. In his book *Real Boys*, William Pollack explains that when we emphasize anger with our sons, they may learn to hide their other feelings. As one father told me, "If my son told his friends how he feels, they'd think he was a sissy." And if boys don't have the opportunity to talk about their sadness and fears, they won't learn to cope with how they feel but will instead learn to ignore, avoid, or even hide such feelings. They'll be less likely to reach out and to help others in distress.

Although boys, in general, are less likely to tell you how they feel than girls are, they do have feelings—and they will talk about them, often during calm, peaceful moments. In my experience, boys of all ages enjoy talking about what makes them proud, sad, frustrated, and afraid—just as much as girls do.

To help avoid sending different messages to boys and girls and trapping our kids in sex-linked stereotypes, Nora Newcombe, a developmental psychologist at Temple University in Philadelphia, Pennsylvania, adds these suggestions to those offered by Newberger and Pollack:

- Encourage your sons as well as your daughters to talk about people's feelings as well as their own.
- Ask questions to boys and girls about how characters feel in storybooks, on TV, and in movies. When you read stories, even to infants, emphasize feeling words—such as happy, sad, and angry—to your sons and daughters, and use appropriate facial expressions and tones of voice. Do this even if your sons don't seem to respond to it or shut down. This is important to help your child develop empathy for others in discomfort and the need to help.
- Talk about all feelings, not just good ones, to your sons as well as to your daughters. Sharing your feelings frees your kids to share theirs.
- Help your child to realize that he may have mixed feelings about things—and then focus on the positive side to help relieve his stress. When you explain how common such ambivalence is, most kids understand. Ten-year-old Ben felt sad and worried when he broke his leg and disappointed that he couldn't play soccer—but he also felt happy about all the attention he was getting.
- Whether you are a mother or father, use supporting, nurturing statements with your sons as well as your daughters.
- Explain to your sons as well as your daughters why hitting others and grabbing toys is unacceptable. Simply punishing boys for aggression may only make them more aggressive.

While we want our boys to know their feelings are important, we want girls to know we value their thoughts. Praise your daughter for her accomplishments and ideas, not just on how she looks.

And when your daughter is talking, try to not interrupt her.

## Parents Have Feelings, Too

Your four-year-old keeps jumping on the couch with his shoes on. You love looking at his happy face; you delight in his exuberance. But you also want him to know that you have feelings, too, and that right now, you're concerned that he'll ruin the sofa cushions. You feel like yelling, "Get off the couch, you'll get it all dirty!" but you also know that yelling doesn't work: your child tunes it out.

Your six-year-old is sitting on the living room rug and finger-painting. You love the fact that she can amuse herself and that she wants to express herself through art. But you've also told her time and time again that she can't paint on the rug, and that wherever she paints, she has to cover the area with newspaper. You have feelings, too. So you sit down with her and explain why you don't want her to paint on the rug. Yet you don't want to squelch her creative energy. You talk. She nods. But you wonder if she heard a word that you said.

What can you do instead? First, assume that your children aren't defying you on purpose. They don't want to dirty the couch cushions or stain your rug with finger paint. They're simply not thinking of you at all. And that's the problem.

Here's how you can involve your child in a conversation that will help him reach his own goals while understanding your point of view:

When a child jumps on the couch, ask, "What might happen if you jump on the couch?"

Some kids might say, "I don't know," or more defiantly, "I don't care."

Try not to get excited, and calmly say, "I know if you think really hard, you can think of something that might happen."

If your child says, "You'll make me go to my room," you can guide him without telling him by asking, "And what could happen if you don't see where you're jumping?" The idea here is for children to recognize why jumping or running inside is not a good idea,

rather than to have them react to the external threat of being yelled at or sent to their room.

Now if your child says, "I might get hurt," or, "I might get something dirty," you can ask, "How might *you* feel about that?" Most children will say, "Sad." Follow that with, "How do you think *I* will feel if that happens?" Most children will say, "Sad," or "Mad." Finally, ask, "Can you think of a *different* place to jump [or paint] so that won't happen, and we both won't feel sad or mad?"

When one dad I know asked his four-year-old daughter these questions, she thought of her own solution: that outside would be a good place to jump—and off she went with a smile on her face. Dad was smiling, too. He recognized his daughter's needs, while she recognized that Dad has feelings, too.

Here's another scenario. Your ten-year-old and seven-year-old are playing tag in the dining room, running for their lives. As they tear through, the vase on the table wobbles and falls to the floor, where it shatters. You're livid. You spank them and send them to their rooms. But that doesn't accomplish very much. Now each boy is angry with the other for getting them both in trouble. They're both mad at you for not understanding that they didn't break the vase on purpose. And you're furious at both of them for being so careless and thoughtless.

If your children actually break something, you can ask the same kinds of questions as above:

"Was the dining room a good place to run?"
"What happened when you ran?"
"How do you feel about what happened?"
"How do you think I feel about it?"
"Where is a good place to play?"
"What are you going to think about the next time you want to play tag inside the house?"

In this way, children will grow accustomed to factoring your needs into their equation. But the problem won't entirely disappear. Many preteens are still oblivious to anyone's needs other than their own. Here's how another dad helped his preteen daughters see that different people can feel different ways about the same thing, by asking them, "How can this be?"

**Dad:** Let's make up a story about two girls your age. Alice loves to play music really *loud*; it makes her feel good. Her sister Mary hears the same music and feels angry. How can this be?

**Emily:** Maybe Alice is remembering how loud the music was at the dance at the school last week. She loves to dance to really loud music.

**Tina:** But if Mary's trying to do her homework, then the music is probably bothering her.

**Dad:** Good thinking. Now you make up a story like mine.

**Emily:** Eve got a soccer ball for her birthday and she felt really happy. Carol got one but she felt scared. Eve loves soccer and Carol is always afraid of getting hit in the head.

**Tina:** Jackie felt proud because she got the lead in the school play. Cindi didn't even want to try out for the part because she's afraid of forgetting her lines.

Both girls now understand that different people can feel different ways about the same thing. When disagreements arise at home, this dad need only remind his daughters of their stories, and ask, "How can this be?" No more usually needs to be said.

You can also play the "How do people feel about things?" game. Here's how:

Start with a good-feeling word, like *happy*. Ask your child, "What makes you happy?" Then ask, "What else? Try to think of five things."

After your child has answered, say, "Now tell me what might make your friend Tom feel happy? How about Grandma? What about Dr. Peters?"

When your child answers, say, "Now we're going to make this game a little harder. What might make your friend, Grandma, and Dr. Peters feel happy?" She may say something like, "An ice-cream cone."

Then ask, "What might make Tom feel happy but not Grandma?" Your child may say, "A video game."

"What would make Grandma feel happy but not Tom?" you can ask next.

"A visit to the museum," your child may say.

Next, you can play the game with other feeling words, like *sad, angry, disappointed,* and *worried.*

Dialogues like these encourage children to develop the capacity to take their own needs and the needs of others into consideration at the same time and to come up with a mutually agreeable solution. It's one of the best ways we can equip our children for all the relationships they'll develop over the course of their lives.

## What Does It Mean to Be "Kind"?

I sometimes think it's easier to teach children what it means to be fair than to be kind. Take, for example, Bobby, age ten, and his sister, Ellie, who's nine. Both kids know that when they play with games, they're each responsible for putting them away. Neither expects the other to do that for him or her.

But as a result of learning this, they've begun to take the idea of fairness too literally, monitoring each other's every move. For example, when it was time for Ellie to straighten up her room, she'd put everything away except the one book her brother had taken off her shelf, adamantly proclaiming, "He put it on the bed so he should put it back!"

Equally adamant, Bobby would take the butter out of the refrigerator but insist that Ellie put it back, because "she was the last one to use it!"

Their dad was bewildered. He agreed that each child had a point but wondered how they had so much energy to keep track of it all. They seemed to be taking the idea of "fairness" to such an extreme. Was it really worth getting so bent out of shape? Fairness, after all, is supposed to spare people's feelings. But for Bobby and Ellie, being "fair" had just the opposite effect.

My own research shows that by the age of four, most kids understand that when one child plays with a toy and the other doesn't, it is fair for the one who played with it to put it away. But it is not until about age nine or ten that kids understand how kindness goes beyond the rules of fairness. That is, both Bobby and Ellie can make the following distinction: that while it's not unfair of her to insist that her brother put the book away, it would be kind of her to do that while she straightens up the room. Similarly, Bobby can realize that although his sister also used the butter, it would be kind of him to put it away.

There is a fine line between fairness and kindness. While we don't want to encourage pettiness, we also don't want to condone irresponsibility. Focusing on the bigger picture—cooperation—instead of the letter of the law may help kids see that sometimes a book on the bed isn't a huge problem worth fighting over, but only a book that can be easily put away. And often, it's wiser to be kind than fair.

But what does it mean to be kind? Does it mean the same thing to children as it does to adults? Al and Clara Baldwin, formerly of Cornell University, examined how youngsters from kindergarten through eighth grade thought about what it means to be kind, and found that sometimes the answer to this question is no.

By age eight, most children agree with adults that a child is nicer when he purposely retrieves a lost ball for a friend than when he accidentally kicks that ball and it ends up in front of the child. But many kindergartners believe that the child was nice both times because the other kid got the ball. That's because they focus not on *how* he got it but *that* he got it.

In a second scenario, most children by age eight agree with adults that a child who gives his brother a toy because he wants to is nicer than a child who does so because his mother asks him to. But again, many kindergartners think the child was nice both times because he gave his brother the toy. Often, very young children do not understand that intention, not result, defines kindness.

Inspired by the Baldwins' research, I asked some kids specific questions to learn how they define kindness. Sally and Margy, both age five, agreed with adults about kindness when intention and choice were the issues. But when we talked about self-sacrifice, Sally and Margy, like many kids their age, thought a different way. For example, many adults believe that a child is kinder when she gives another child a toy she is playing with than when she gives someone a toy she is not playing with. But Sally and Margy believe that giving a toy she is not using is kinder.

Sally's dad then said to his daughter: "Suppose your friend forgot to bring her dancing shoes to dance class. Which would be the kinder thing to do: to offer your friend your own shoes, or to give her the extra pair that you happened to bring with you?" Sally thought she would be nicer if she gave her the extra pair, not sacrificing her only pair—"'cause then both get to dance." Again, Sally was focusing on the end result rather than the reason for the act—in this case, self-sacrifice.

Freddi, eleven, agreed with adults that it is nicer to do a favor for someone and not expect something in return than it is when you expect the person to return the favor. But Freddi added an interesting twist: "If she keeps giving kids things and never gets nothing back, she'd be considered a dork and people would take advantage of her."

Clearly, children may not always think the same way we do about what is kind. When we get angry with our kids because we think they're uncaring, or, as we have also seen, when they sacrifice kindness for fairness, we might think about what it really means to our kids when we ask them to "be nice."

## "Now Say You're Sorry!"—but Does She Really Mean It?

Your four-year-old grabs a toy from her sister; your five-year-old calls a visiting friend a name; your six-year-old hits his younger brother. There are many ways to change these kinds of behavior in kids. One common way is to say, "That's not nice. Now say you're sorry."

Your child may quickly comply and say she's sorry—and you may think that's the end of it. But is it?

Other children say, "I'm sorry" automatically. They hit or tease others, and then avoid being yelled at by apologizing. Children learn quickly that this is often their ticket out of punishment.

Ask yourself: Does your child feel genuine empathy? Is he really sad inside that he might have hurt someone or made someone feel bad? That's the goal, not a parroting of your own words. Saying, "I'm sorry" when told to comes from the outside. Kids who think about their own and others' feelings *won't want* to hurt themselves or others. That comes from the inside.

To help kids learn empathy, ask your child how her friends or siblings feel when she grabs, hits, or teases them.

One four-year-old surprised me when he replied, "I feel sad when I hurt my brother."

Follow that by asking, "What can you do so you won't feel sad?"

The same lesson applies to situations like stealing. Sometimes children get in the habit of lifting things—they take a necklace from their sister's room or some money from your bureau. Shelly, age eleven, often took pens and other small objects from her classmates without their permission. Each time she was caught, she was sent to the principal's office and given detention. One day, she told her teacher that she wouldn't steal anymore because she didn't want to get caught. Her teacher was thrilled. So was her principal. But I wasn't.

I believed that the teacher and principal were focusing on the wrong half of the sentence—the fact that Shelly said she wouldn't steal anymore. While that's a start, it demonstrated that Shelly was still only thinking of herself and what would happen to her. She was not thinking of her victim, or how that person would feel. I had to wonder if Shelly would gladly steal again if she could figure out a way to do so without getting caught.

---

Saying, "I'm sorry" when told to comes from the outside. Kids who think about their own and others' feelings *won't want* to hurt themselves or others. That comes from the inside.

---

How can Shelly learn to empathize with her victims and not just think about herself? We can ask her these questions:

"What might happen if you take people's things without asking them?"
"How do they feel about that?"
"How would you feel if that happened to you?"

And, if appropriate:

"What might happen if your classmate didn't have the book [or other stolen item] she needed to do her homework?"

Children as young as age four can appreciate that taking things hurts someone. When I have asked them, "What might happen if a child took his mom's umbrella when she wasn't looking?" some kids simply say, "She'll be mad," "I'll get spanked," or "She'll say, 'Stealing isn't nice.'"

Others were able to appreciate that "Mom will get wet if it rains." Aren't the kids who think about the victims less likely to hurt others, even if they never get caught?

These children have learned the true meaning of empathy. One way your child can learn this is to show him that you can misinterpret his behavior, and let him know how you really feel when that happens. Nine-year-old Jason's mom had an opportunity to do just that. He was spending the day with her at her office. Predictably, he became antsy during the midmorning and began to vie for her attention. Mom tried to explain that she was very busy and suggested he go into the next room to read some of the books he had brought. Jason said, "I'm sorry," and dutifully retreated.

Mom thought her son understood that his pestering was keeping her from her work, and she was pleased that he so compliantly left her alone. But Jason interpreted this a completely different way. He thought her "chasing" him away meant, "Her work is more important than me."

Jason thought of a unique way to solve this problem. Instead of reading his book, he wrote his mom a letter, telling her he didn't mean to keep her from doing her work but just wanted to talk to her for a little while. While putting his thoughts on paper, Jason came to realize that his mom really did have work to do—that's why she was there—and he needed a way to mesh his needs with hers. He put all these thoughts into the letter.

When Mom read the letter she was very touched and began to see Jason's behavior in a new way. "Maybe I'm not paying enough attention to my son," she thought to herself. She suggested that they have a special talk over lunch. At that time, Mom let Jason know she felt genuinely sorry for appearing to be ignoring him. And Jason sincerely apologized for bothering his mom. During this talk, Jason came to understand his mom's needs, just as his mom came to understand his.

Kids who *feel* sorry can think about the feelings and viewpoints of others. Those who just *say* "I'm sorry" are thinking of themselves and are complying to get rid of us nagging, demanding adults. Is that what we really want?

## Help Kids Be Helpers and Give as They Receive

Does your child appreciate the value of money? Does he spend his allowance too quickly and then want more? Do hassles over money become a major source of conflict between you and your child?

Some families find it difficult to talk about money. But the sooner your child begins to understand its value and meaning, the better.

Jamie, eight, is learning how to appreciate the value of money the old-fashioned way. He earns it. His parents are very creative about this.

Every birthday, Jamie is asked to choose three toys he doesn't play with anymore and to put them by the door. They wait three days, telling Jamie he can change his mind about any or all of them.

His parents then say, "You're going to be getting new toys for your birthday. Do you think other children might like to play with the toys you don't play with anymore?"

When Jamie agrees, they all take the toys to a consignment store.

If the toys are sold, they go back to the store, pick up the check, go to the bank, and deposit the money in Jamie's account. His parents have explained about saving money for things he wants, now and later.

They've been doing this since Jamie was six. What I especially like about this plan is that it not only teaches Jamie about saving money and about planning for the future, but he's also learning about giving.

There are many other ways to help your child think about earning, saving, and helping others. Often, the holidays are a good time of year to encourage this kind of thinking. If your child, like Jamie, is used to the idea of recycling toys, then it's a small step to suggesting that he take the clothes he's outgrown and donate them to an organization that clothes the needy, or that he suggest that his class bring in a can and make a donation to the local food pantry. Whatever your child decides to do, talk about the people he or she is helping. You might want to discuss why some people are in wheelchairs, or why some people need the gift of clothes from people they don't know. You can even talk about why some people may be homeless.

Let your child suggest people who are in need of help and why they may need help. This kind of talk encourages empathy—the capacity to genuinely care about others less fortunate than oneself. And no child is too young. Even a four-year-old can draw a special picture to bring to a relative who is in the hospital. You can talk to your child about what hobbies people have, or what they do at work, or if they love a special food. Then, your child can think about what to draw or write for them, even if it's just a scribble.

One holiday season, my cousin's seven-year-old daughter had a present for me. Because she knew I love tennis, she wrote me this story: "Myrna's secret dream was to be a tennis ball, but she was afraid it would hurt when she got hit. So she made a big tennis ball she could fit into so she won't feel it when she gets hit. Then she met a man in a tennis-racket suit and they played together forever."

This story meant so much to me—because I knew she was thinking of me.

Children feel good about themselves when they see that others are touched by the gifts they give. You'll feel proud of your child, too.

## Help Your Child Understand Those with Disabilities

Perhaps your child knows someone, a classmate or a neighbor, for instance, with a physical or neurological disability. Does he feel uncomfortable to see a child in a wheelchair or on crutches? Does he stare if someone displays uncontrollable behaviors such as muscular tics? Or is your child unfazed by these conditions? Would he want to be the disabled child's friend?

Most likely, the more time your child spends with the child who is disabled, the more comfortable he feels. When kids get to know each other and engage in fun activities together, they realize how alike they are. In Philadelphia, a unique program was designed to make this happen. Third- and fourth-grade students from the HMS School for Children with Cerebral Palsy are paired with children from the Germantown Friends School

(GFS), an independent Quaker school, to rehearse together for a musical performance. "This partnership allows children to see what youngsters with physical disabilities can do, and not focus only on what they cannot do," says Mindy Olimpi, HMS student services coordinator.

When I attended a rehearsal, I saw for myself how children from the two different schools related and worked side by side. Youngsters in wheelchairs twirled in rhythm to the sounds, sometimes aided by children without disabilities, sometimes alone; they also sang or, if they were unable to sing, made sounds with an assistive communicative device. But it wasn't so much what they did that struck me. It was watching the smiles and laughter of the children, and how the partners connected with each other. I could sense a bond between many of the pairs, and how much that bond meant to each of them.

But this bonding did not always come so easily. Erica, a ten-year-old student from GFS, felt "a little scared at first," but soon came to appreciate that kids from HMS "have to deal with stuff every day. They watch other kids and they think, 'I can't do what they do.' That must be hard. Now I feel less afraid." She learned that HMS kids can do many things—draw, for example, in art class, if not with their hands, then with their toes. Most HMS kids know their numbers and letters. She also learned to appreciate what she can do as well, and has become aware of how her own classmates feel when they are made fun of.

Students at HMS appreciated the experience, too. Rhonda, twelve, felt nervous about the kids from GFS coming to visit because "at first I didn't know if they would like me." But after she talked about her feelings, she felt better. She loves the exchange because "I get to be a part of something and socialize a little more." With a winning smile, Rhonda continued, "I love this and I love to sing and dance." But most important, she added, "We can do stuff like other kids. We're just regular kids."

With classrooms becoming increasingly mainstreamed nationwide, it is quite possible that your child is in daily contact with a peer who has a physical or neurological disability. To help her care, and feel comfortable, you can ask such questions as:

> "What do you think that child is thinking about when she comes to school?"

"How do the kids in your class treat her?"
"How do you think she feels about that?"
"What can you do or say if she needs help?"

Questions like these helped Lily, age eleven, whose classmate Doug has Tourette's syndrome, a neurological disorder characterized by involuntary muscle twitches, tics, or vocalizations that occur rapidly and frequently. Not only do some kids call Doug "Rubber Face" when his muscles twitch, but they also complain that he sings too loud and sings the same thing every time. "Oh no, not again!" one classmate always exclaims at music time when Doug starts to sing.

After Lily considered the questions above, she felt more sympathy for Doug and said to her classmate, "It's not fair. Give him a chance. Maybe he'll sing something different today." Hearing this vote of confidence bolstered Doug's determination: he managed to sing at least five notes of a new song. He then shook Lily's hand and smiled. With just one more reminder from Lily, the kids stopped teasing Doug.

Whether through an organized program like the HMS-GFS partnership in Philadelphia, or by helping children think about how others think and feel, children without disabilities can come to realize that children with disabilities have the same thoughts, feelings, and hopes—and are basically the same inside.

After talking with Erica, Rhonda, and Lily, I was very moved. You will be, too, if you help your child reach out to those who are living with challenges we may not at first understand.

# 6

# Self-Esteem and Sense of Control

## To Praise or Not to Praise

Your six-year-old drew a picture of a dog. When he shows it to you, you say, "That's beautiful. You're a real artist."

Your ten-year-old got a perfect grade on his math test. You say, "You're so smart."

Your twelve-year-old scored a goal for her soccer team during the first game she played. You say, "Great job! I'm so proud of you."

These responses are all natural. When we see our children proud of their achievements, we feel proud, too. We want to reinforce their behavior. That's what gives them the incentive to try again and to persist.

But does this kind of praise really make your kids feel good? The answer is a little more complicated than you might expect.

On the one hand, of course it does. We all love to hear praise, and kids need to feel good about their accomplishments.

But too much praise can backfire. Instead of making kids feel good about themselves, they can end up more worried. Suppose Jamal gets 100 on a math test, and his parents say things like, "You're so smart. I'm so proud of you." That's a lot to live up to. He may begin to worry about what's expected of him. "What if I only get a 90 next time, or an 80?" he may think to himself. "Will my parents still think I'm so smart?"

"When I was a kid," one mom told me, "my parents always told me how smart and beautiful and creative I was. By the time I was ten, I was afraid to try anything new. I stuck to doing things I knew I could do. It was less risky. I was too afraid that I'd fail and feel bad about myself—and disappoint my parents, too."

Also, kids have a real sensitivity for what they perceive are false statements. When you say to your child, "You're a real artist," you're being sincere even though you may be exaggerating. But children can be very literal. Your child may think to herself, "What is she talking about? I know what an artist is—they're people who draw pictures in books. I'm not as good as that!" Then, your child will start to distrust what you say.

But perhaps the most insidious problem with too much praise is that children start performing to please you instead of themselves. They become motivated by extrinsic factors—your praise—rather than by their own desire to do well, or by their own enjoyment of what they're doing.

Here are some different ways you can talk to your child about her accomplishments so that she feels rewarded:

"You've really worked very hard. How do you feel about what you did?"
"Tell me more about your picture [or the test, or the game]."
"What were you thinking about when you drew the dog [or took the test or scored the goal]?"

What you're trying to do, by making comments like these, is to focus your child's attention on her feelings and thoughts rather than on her accomplishment. By emphasizing the process rather than the product, your child will come to realize that it's the trying that counts.

Offering a quick fix of praise may be a hard habit to break. But the next time you feel like automatically saying, "That's great!"—stop yourself. Instead, let your child tell you about what he's done and how he feels. It will be better for both of you.

## A Niche for Every Kid

Do you have a child who excels at music, who can play any instrument he picks up? Is he academically gifted? Is she a star athlete?

Perhaps you have another child who does not excel, who enjoys fewer accolades, and never seems to be the star of anything. If you do, you're probably worried that he or she feels jealous of his more talented sibling.

I recently met Beth, a ten-year-old girl who was an A student, pitched on her softball team, and played piano. Yet she wasn't happy, mostly because she was very envious of her younger brother, a violinist so talented he was taking lessons with a master teacher.

Beth's parents knew she was special, but didn't know how to help her realize it. Here are some suggestions for helping every child understand this.

Rather than having your child follow in his illustrious sibling's footsteps, encourage him to find a different hobby, instrument, art, or field of interest at school. Sometimes helping your child with a special project, like one for a science fair, for instance, can spark his interest in the subject. Be creative when you think about options. If the usual baseball and football don't interest your child, introduce him to other wonderful sports such as tennis, bowling, golf, or fencing.

Let your child know she doesn't have to be perfect. What you want is for her to find an activity that enables her to feel good about herself. Putting too much pressure on her to "be good," to win, or to practice every day, no matter what, can have the opposite effect—she'll begin to feel bad about the activity and about herself, and lose interest in it.

What Beth's parents did was take her to the local Y on a Saturday morning so she could have a tour and see all the different classes taking place. She felt herself drawn to the pottery studio, so her parents signed her up for a class. Now the pottery studio is the place Beth most loves to be: her face lights up whenever it's time for her to go. She's not worried about preparing or about being the best; she just loves creating things. More important, thanks to pottery, she met a whole new group of kids and found some new friends.

Beth found her niche. Now, when she hears her brother practicing the violin, she doesn't feel eaten up with envy. She thinks about the next pot she's going to throw on her wheel. Her own creative juices are flowing.

# "Does Anybody Care About Me?"

We all want our kids to be caring, sharing human beings who don't want to hurt other people. But too much attention to teaching our kids to share and to pay attention to how others feel can have the opposite effect of what you want—it can make them wonder if anyone cares about them.

When four-year-old Evan hit his brother, his mom said, "Evan, you can't hit Roy. Roy doesn't like to be hit. Now say you're sorry." Dutifully, Evan apologized.

Another mom walked into her six-year-old son's room just when he was grabbing his toy away from his friend. This mom said, "You should share your toys." Now her son is upset. He thought he had been sharing his toy—the problem was that his friend wouldn't give the toy back.

Both moms thought that they were teaching their sons to pay attention to the feelings of others. But in each case, both boys were left feeling bad about their own feelings.

Before turning your child's attention to how another person is feeling, focus on *his* feelings. To find out what's on his mind, ask a few questions:

> "What happened right before you hit your brother [or before you grabbed the toy]?"
> "What happened next?"
> "How did you feel when you started to argue?"

Asking a child how he feels is a very dynamic question. If we want our kids to care about others, they have to first care about themselves. Children whose needs are satisfied and can relieve their own tensions with support from Mom and Dad are not preoccupied with unmet needs and can pay attention to others' emotions. They can give to and do things for others because they feel cared about, safe, and secure. And as Nancy Eisenberg, author of *The Caring Child*, tells us, these children are more empathic, more popular, and have a higher self-esteem.

Here are some ways to show your child you genuinely care about him:

- Avoid discipline techniques that will frighten or anger your child. Yelling, threatening, and other overpowering approaches will make it difficult for your child to attend to your thoughts and feelings. Additionally, because he's under such stress, he will not be able to focus on your directions for what you want him to do.
- Share your own thoughts and feelings about things, now and from your own childhood. You'll show your child that considering your own feelings is important, and that it's important for him to think about his feelings, too.
- Respect your child's needs. As illustrated by Paul Light, author of *The Development of Social Sensitivity*, a child who explains that he cannot comply with your request at a given moment because he's in the middle of something, and then hears, "Do it now!" can easily believe that Mom doesn't care about him and places her needs over his. If you think your child is genuinely busy, and not using that as an excuse to procrastinate, let him know he can do what you ask when he's finished with what he's involved in at the moment. You don't like to be interrupted when you're busy. Neither does your child.

It might be, however, that your child is merely being thoughtless. One six-year-old was wrapped up in her video game and ignored Mom's statement that dinner was ready. She appeared unconcerned that the whole family was waiting for her. If this is the case, you can ask, "What might happen if you don't come to dinner now?"

If she answers, "I won't get dinner," something she may have heard before, ask, "What else might happen?" Try to guide your child to a more empathic consequence. To help her, you can ask, "What might happen to the food if we wait too long to eat it?" You can add, "We like to eat together as a family. We like it when you join us. How might the rest of us feel if we have to wait too long to eat?" Then add, "How would *you* feel if that happens?"

Children who feel that "no one cares" about them can also feel that they are "not important" and have low self-esteem. To gain attention, they may lash out and hurt others, more concerned about themselves than the person they hurt. Or they may withdraw and turn inward, fearful of approaching others who "don't care." It is also possible that they will just remain thoughtless, and continue not to care about others who don't care about them.

To help your child feel comfortable with her own feelings, which paves the way for her concern about others, ask her how she feels about things, even when she's the one who yells or remains unconcerned about others. You'll send her a very important message: "I care about how you feel and I want you to care, too."

## "I Can Make It Happen!"

Do you believe that good things happen to you because you have worked hard to make them happen or because you had a stroke of good luck?

If someone is ignoring you, do you try to figure out why, or assume that there's nothing you can do to change it?

Those of us who attribute our success to luck, or to conditions beyond our control rather than to our own efforts, are less likely to strive for what we want in life. Similarly, those of us who blame our failures on others, or the situation, instead of taking action, are likely to give up too soon, believing that what happens is outside of our control.

The same is true for our kids. Let's look at four sixth-graders who had to prepare a science project. Two received high marks and two received low marks, but each attributed the grade differently.

John got an A on his science project and felt great about it. He knew it was because he worked hard and earned the grade.

Ben also got an A, but he assumed he got the grade because the project was easy. Ben couldn't feel the same sense of pride as John because he didn't believe he had had anything to do with his success.

Susan received an F for the project, but she felt the grade was fair: she realized that she hadn't spent enough time preparing it.

Cody also received an F, but she believed that she failed because the assignment was too hard and because the teacher—whom she believed never liked her—wasn't a fair grader. In short, Cody thought the deck was stacked against her—that there was nothing she could have done to get a better grade.

Though John and Susan received very disparate grades on their projects, they both came to the same realization: whatever the outcome, they know that they can act to make things happen. Ben and Cody, on the other hand, believe things just happen to them.

There are some things in life we really can't control. But we can handle even these acts of nature in different ways. For instance, Richard was disappointed when a major snowstorm canceled his soccer game, but he planned his day at home so that he could get many things done and felt satisfied when it was over. His teammate Bill pouted and whined the whole day away because, as he put it, "Things just never go right."

Researchers Stephen Nowicki and Marshall Duke suggest that kids who take an active role in their lives feel better about themselves, try harder to reach their goals, get frustrated less easily, and have more friends. They also do better in school. Wendy Roedell, Ron Slaby, and Halbert Robinson explain that kids who have a feeling of control spend more time doing homework and, when a task is difficult, don't give up easily.

My own research, which I conducted with my colleagues George Spivack and Jerry Platt, suggests that youngsters who can think of strategies to solve problems that arise with peers and figures of authority are more likely to be successful and to feel more in control of their lives. On the other hand, perhaps children who feel incompetent and cannot make things happen will also retreat from helping others because they believe they lack the necessary skills to do so. It may be that these children have a limited repertoire of solutions available to them, and when these fail, they feel powerless because they have no further options.

Here's how you can help your kids believe they can make things happen:

- Let them know when they do something well, but do so without showering them with so much praise that they begin to worry about letting you down or performing only to please you.
- Let them make their own decisions whenever possible so they will recognize their role in what occurs and try harder to make good choices.
- Help them to try to think of more ways to reach their goals if their first ideas should fail.

Help your child appreciate how his efforts produce results, and what else he might do when he doesn't achieve a desired outcome. This will help him believe that he can make things happen—instead of believing that things always happen to him.

■

# PART 2

# Handling and Preventing Problems

*Children who can solve problems important to them now*
*will be able to solve problems important to them later.*

You ask your daughter to help with the dishes but she says no, and when you ask her again she talks back in ways that drive you to distraction. Your son gets frustrated when things don't go his way and can't wait for what he wants, yet he can wait forever to do what you want him to do.

Sound familiar? These behaviors and others like them are, up to a point, normal. Most children spend a lot of time feeling their oats and testing your limits.

But these behaviors can prove awfully annoying. Even more worrisome is the fact that if left unchecked, they sometimes lead to a more serious form of aggression that leaves kids socially isolated. And children who are aggressive, impatient, and impulsive can be at risk for experimenting with drugs, indulging in unsafe sex, and engaging in violent behavior when they are older.

Certainly not all children who act in these ways will end up having more serious problems. Still, it's important to nip these behaviors in the bud. It will not only make for a happier childhood, but it may also create a strong new kind of bond between you and your child that will prepare her for the teen years—when she begins to confront more complex issues.

In Part 1, I talked about helping children learn to identify, express, and cope with their feelings, and how they can use those emotions to help them take control of their lives. That sets the stage for Part 2, in which I'll show you how children can learn to use those skills in everyday life. Once they do, not only will they be less likely to act out in annoying ways, but they will also be less at risk for developing more serious problems when they are older.

I'll consider different arenas in which conflicts often erupt. Fights about bedtime, when to begin a book report due a week from now, and choosing the right moment to ask for a favor are all about timing. Another familiar topic for kids to argue over is possessiveness: how to share toys, time, and living space. For kids to understand why they shouldn't tattle on each other or lie, they need to explore the notions of truthfulness and helpfulness. And then there is defiance, which seems to increase as children grow. If you find yourself saying, "Don't get sassy with me!" too many times, you'll be particularly interested in this section. To address all these issues, children need to learn to consider the situation from the other person's point of view.

There's also a chapter on physical aggression—how to handle the situation when a child hits another child, pushes, grabs a toy, or in other ways physically harms or intends to harm someone—as well as verbal confrontations, when a child teases, insults, or calls another names.

Recently, another form of aggression has come to our attention—one that interferes with relationships between people. It happens when people talk behind one's back, spread rumors, or exclude kids from parties or the lunch table. This kind of purposeful manipulation or damage to peer relationships, coined "relational aggression" by psychologist Nicki Crick and her colleagues at the University of Minnesota, begins at age eight or nine (though its precursors can appear as early as the preschool years), occurs more in girls than in boys, and is less visible than acts of physical or verbal aggression. Teachers and parents are not always aware of this "underground" behavior. Yet this kind of emotional aggression can be as painful—if not more so—than getting kicked in the shins. This kind of pain lasts longer because it hurts inside. And when kids feel bad inside, they may come to dislike themselves and, in time, won't want to go to school.

Why are some youngsters driven to overpower or torment weaker peers who do not, or cannot, defend themselves? Some are trying to earn respect the only way they know how—through intimidation. Some may have a need to regain control taken away from them. This often happens in homes where discipline is so harsh and extreme that kids relieve their frustration by taking it out on safer, less powerful peers at school. Some may have been bullied themselves and use aggression as a form of revenge.

And what happens to the victims of aggression—those who are attacked physically, verbally, or emotionally? Not only do they suffer in misery during their years in school, but beyond—perhaps for a lifetime, reports educator John Hoover. In fact, Peter Smith and his colleagues found that youngsters who were threatened, humiliated, belittled, or otherwise picked on in school—especially those who did not, and still don't, have coping strategies—may continue to be victimized years later in the workplace.

Both bullies and their victims must be noticed. Crick and others such as Patricia Brennan and her colleagues have found that bullying and the effects of bullying do not go away by themselves, and both the perpetrators and the persecuted often suffer later psychological disorders such as anxiety or depression, or act out and become delinquents. According to researcher Tonja Nansel and her colleagues, an average of one in seven American schoolchildren—that's almost five million kids—is either a bully, the victim of one, or both. No wonder the youngsters I interviewed for my book *Raising a Thinking Preteen* mentioned being bullied as their number one concern. Their parents are worried, too—not so much that their child will be the bully but rather the victim of one. And many times, the victimized remain fearful and silent.

What can you do? Plenty. Swedish psychologists Hakan Stattin and Margaret Kerr found that parents' reactions to their children's behavior can play a key role in stemming the trend toward aggression and violence. They pinpoint three ways parents can monitor their children:

1. Parents can impose rules and restrictions on their child and his or her activities and associations. But this approach could cause children to become secretive about what they do.
2. Parents can ask their child or their child's friends for information. But children often perceive these questions as infringing on their privacy.
3. Children can spontaneously tell their parents, without any prompting, what's on their minds, a behavior called child disclosure.

The results are clear: the more a child voluntarily and spontaneously discloses information, the more parents will know of their child's behavior. In addition, children who disclose also engage in fewer risk-taking and antisocial activities. These researchers conclude that a good parent-child relationship should be a two-way process, of reciprocity and cooperation, where adolescents develop "trust in their parents" and "feel that their parents are willing to listen to them, are responsive, and would not ridicule or punish if they confided in them."

In these chapters, you'll see why some children are comfortable talking to their parents, while others aren't. I hope that you'll also conclude, as I did, that the difference between children who experiment with alcohol, tobacco, and drugs, or who succumb to aggression and violence, and those who remain unscathed, even if they grow up in dire circumstances, has to do with the way children think. If children know what it means to hurt themselves and others, they will be less likely to cause harm. It is this awareness that I want to teach.

I will also show you how to use problem-solving methods when you talk with your children about annoying and early high-risk behaviors. After these conversations, the wall of silence often begins to crumble. When parents encourage trust, children respond by confiding in their parents, sharing what they're doing, where they're going, and with whom they're doing it.

Children who can solve problems important to them now will be able to prevent problems from escalating out of control later—in middle school, high school, and beyond.

# 7

# Time and Timing: Bedtime, Procrastination, Interrupting, Impatience

## "Is This a Good Time?"—"What Can I Do While I Wait?"

Your five-year-old takes out his finger paints just as you're getting his gear ready to go to the park.

Your eight-year-old wants you to color with her the moment you sit down to pay the monthly bills. When you ask her to wait, she whines, "You *never* help me."

Your eleven-year-old begins to dial her friend's phone number just as you take the roast for dinner out of the oven.

What can you do? What do you say? You want to be there for your child, but you'd like her to be more sensitive to your needs, too. And you want her to pay more attention to what's going on around her so that she's not thinking only of herself.

To address these important issues, I created a game called the "Good-Time/Not-Good-Time" game, which children enjoy. Play it anytime during the day—only not right after a situation like the ones above arise—and use fictitious characters. If your children are familiar with the game, they will be able to apply its lessons to real life.

Here's how one mom played this game with her nine- and eleven-year-old daughters.

**Mom:** Let's play the "Good-Time/Not-Good-Time" game. Listen carefully. Joanie asks her friend Patricia to join her and her friends for a game of soccer—only Patricia has just broken her leg. Is that a good time or not a good time to ask Patricia to play soccer?

**Lisa:** That's silly. Not a good time.

**Mom:** Yeah, let's be silly. You make up a not-good-time one.

**Lisa:** Roseann asks her mom to help her with her homework—at three o'clock in the morning.

**Mom:** Good, Lisa. Now it's your turn, Bernice.

**Bernice:** Deedee asked her friend if she could borrow her sweater right after her friend's mom yelled at her friend.

**Mom:** Good thinking, kids. Lisa, when *is* a good time to ask Mom to help you with your homework?

**Lisa:** After school or after dinner.

**Mom:** And Bernice, when is a good time to ask a friend for a favor?

**Bernice:** When she's in a good mood.

Let your kids make up some more silly and not-silly scenarios like the ones above. Then, when they want something while you're busy or at some other inopportune time, you can remind them of the "Good-Time/Not-Good-Time" game.

Even when kids do think about good and not-good times, it might be hard for them to wait for a good time to come. Typically children want what they want *now*. This is quite normal but often drives parents nuts.

Trying to explain to kids that they should learn patience doesn't have much effect—they're too impatient to listen to our explanations. And when we tell kids they can have or do what they want "later," it seems like an eternity to them—because they don't think about what they can do while they wait.

The "What Can You Do While You Wait?" game helps children learn not to be so impatient. Again, start playing the game with fictitious characters.

"Johnny wanted his brother to play checkers with him, but his brother is finishing his math homework," said Arthur's mother to her ten-year-old son. "Can you think of five things Johnny can do while he waits?"

Arthur compiled this list with ease. He answered that Johnny could:

- Do his own homework
- Play a video game
- Eat a snack
- Draw pictures
- Practice his flute

Since that was so easy, Arthur volunteered more:

- He could call a friend.
- He could go online.
- He could organize his stamp collection.

The next time Arthur wanted his mother's attention at an inconvenient time, she was able to say to him, "I can't talk to you right now because I'm helping your sister with her homework. What can you do while you wait?"

Arthur thought for a moment and smiled—he remembered the game. "I guess I can do my homework, too," he said.

You can play these games with children as young as four. Janey, who had just turned four, wanted to go to the playground right after breakfast, but her mom had to sort the laundry. "What can you do while you wait?" her mom asked.

"I'll play with my new doll," Janey said, skipping off to her room to get her doll. She ended up dressing the doll for the playground and taking her along when her mother was ready.

These games are also helpful when the first guest arrives for a birthday or a holiday party with a brightly wrapped gift and your child shouts, in great anticipation, "Can I open it *now*?" If you'd prefer to wait for all the guests to arrive, you can ask your child to think about why now is *not a good time* and then ask, "What can you do while you wait?"

When children come up with their own ideas, as Lisa, Bernice, Arthur, and Janey did, they don't whine. There's no need to—they're busy devising alternatives rather than impatiently fixating on what they can't have at the moment.

## End the Bedtime Wars

Some children toddle off to bed without a whimper—they seem to enjoy the dark, their beds, and bedtime rituals. Other children cling to daylight, ferociously fighting bedtime and sleep. "Just five more minutes," they plead—but this inevitably becomes twenty minutes, then thirty, then more.

Do you read him one more book, allow him to finish that last video game, or grant him that one more wish, whatever that may be? If you do, you're probably growing more resentful each night and wishing for a new strategy. Or do you find yourself yelling, "Go to sleep right now!" or threatening, "If you don't go to sleep now, you'll have no TV tomorrow!" or, "You'll fail your test if you end up falling asleep in school." This is the last thing you want to do. At the end of a long day, children need your warmth, not anger and threats. The more agitated you become, the less relaxed he'll feel and the harder it will be for him to drop off to sleep.

Here are a few suggestions.

First, try to figure out what's really bothering your child. Does she have enough leeway time before lights-out? With a three- or four-year-old, you may want to start the whole routine of bathing, brushing teeth, and changing into PJs much earlier than you have in the past. If you find yourself rushing through the last storybook or TV show before bed, begin these activities earlier as well—turning off a program before the end is much more frustrating to your child than not starting it at all. Let older children plan how much time they need for their nightly routine so that they start at a time you agree on—and that includes getting homework done. And if your child resists sleep because she wants more time with you, then try planning together how and when you'll spend time together each night—this activity alone may give your child the very attention she's been seeking at the end of the day.

If your child still wants to stay up beyond her bedtime, here are some new ideas on how to talk to her about this.

In the morning, ask her how she feels. If she says, "Tired," ask, "What can you do tonight so you won't feel tired in the morning?"

She may say, "Go to bed earlier." But be prepared: come evening, she may forget about this conversation and beg for an additional thirty minutes to read. That's when you ask, "Do you remember our conversation this morning, when you said that the way you could feel less tired in the morning was by going to bed earlier than you did last night?"

If your child balks, you can ask, "How will you feel in the morning if you don't go to sleep now?" You may have to repeat this conversation several mornings and evenings in a row until your child makes the connection. Eventually, most children get the idea.

Once your child understands the connection, you can ask good-time/not-good-time questions:

"Is this a good time or not a good time to go to sleep?"
"Is it a good idea or not a good idea to go to sleep on time?"
"What might happen in school tomorrow if you are tired?"
"Do you want that to happen?"
"When is a good time to read your book?"

When eight-year-old Jen was asked these questions, she said, "If I'm tired tomorrow, I may not do so well on my spelling test."

"Do you want that to happen?" her mom asked.

This time Jen just smiled. "I better go to bed on time tonight," she said.

What about the child who insists, "But I'm not tired!" Consider for a moment that maybe he's telling the truth—in which case he may be ready for a later bedtime.

Most children, however, just refuse to admit to their tiredness. The more you try to explain that they will feel tired tomorrow if they don't go to sleep now, the more defiant they become. If your child really is tired, let him think about that. Hammering it in won't change the way he's acting.

Sometimes, having an older sibling at home adds a new dimension to the bedtime wars, as I can personally attest. When I was six, I suddenly noticed that my twelve-year-old brother got to stay up later than I did. For a while, I genuinely believed that my parents wanted me tucked away so they and my brother could enjoy one another's company without me. My parents tried explaining that he was older and didn't need as much sleep as I did, and that when I got older, I could stay up later, too. But nothing satisfied me. Finally, my dad said, "OK, Myrna, go to bed when your brother does. See how you'll feel."

"I'll be just fine," I said, sounding very sure of myself. And I did feel fine—until the next morning, when I had to wake up.

"How did you feel this morning when you woke up?" Dad asked me at dinner.

I didn't even have to answer. He saw that he wouldn't have to remind me to go to bed on time anymore.

## "I'll Do It Later"—Curing Procrastination

Procrastination seems to come naturally to many children. No matter what you ask them—to clean their rooms, finish their chores, or do their homework—the answer is always the same: "I'll do it later." Most of us are guilty of this sometimes. But when does it become a problem and what can we do about it?

Twelve-year-old Lizzie wanted to be goalie on her soccer team, but she couldn't try out until she had a complete physical. Whenever her mom tried to schedule an appointment with the doctor, Lizzie would say, "Not today." The deadline for physicals passed, and Lizzie couldn't join the team.

Ten-year-old Randi didn't start her major social studies project until the night before it was due, even though it had been assigned two weeks earlier. Her dad reminded her to get started on it every night, but she tuned him out. She received an F.

Four-year-old Thad promised to clean his room right after his video game was over, but he kept on playing. His mom threatened to take the video system away if his room wasn't cleaned up before dinner. But come six o'clock, not one toy had been picked up.

If your child behaves this way, you may be feeling desperate. You may even be tempted to accomplish the task yourself—but resist the temptation. If you end up doing the work, your child will believe that her procrastination paid off. On the other hand, if you try to ignore the fact that she's procrastinating, she may come to believe that ignoring what she has to do will make it go away.

Presented below are some tips for combating the procrastination problem.

First, talk to your child about what happened as a consequence of her procrastination. In Lizzie's case, her delaying tactics resulted in a bitter disappointment for her, and a conversation with her mother about how to meet important deadlines was all it took for Lizzie to resolve to change her behavior.

Randi needed to learn how to complete long-term assignments. With her parents' help, she began planning her homework time so that she worked on assignments due in the future, not just the next day. (For more on planning homework time, see Chapter 18.)

Another helpful way to guide procrastinators is to break the task into small steps. For example, instead of suggesting, "Why don't you put away the toys near your bed first?" (which is an example of thinking for your child), you can ask, "What part of the job do you want to do first? Second?" Even preschoolers can decide for themselves what to do first, or when to do it. Older children can make signs, write themselves notes, or check off days on a calendar to keep track of when their work needs to be finished.

It's possible that some children procrastinate because the task is genuinely unpleasant for them. If your child never takes out the garbage, it may be that he hates the smell of the garbage can. In this case, you may want to agree on another household chore that he can perform.

It's also possible that your child is procrastinating as a way of asserting power, of showing you who's really in control. (Remember, he may be completely unaware of his motivation, but that doesn't mean it's not the case.) In the end, you cannot force him to do his chores or complete his homework. You may want to think about how you talk to him when he doesn't do what you ask. If he feels too controlled, he may feel a need to gain some measure of control back.

If your child continues to put things off, ask him how he feels about the task he's letting go. Some chronic procrastinators are afraid of failing. In these cases, they need to hear, "You don't have to be perfect."

You can tell him about times you tried something new and failed, or didn't do as well as you'd hoped. You may also say, "It's OK to try new things, even if they don't turn out just right. You can always try again. Or try something new." With this reassurance, your child will feel a lot less stress, and you will, too.

## "Can't You See I'm on the Phone!"

You're on the phone—with your boss, your best friend, your favorite great-aunt, your stockbroker—or you're writing out the monthly checks, or taking out the garbage, or washing your hair, and you hear your child say, "Mom, I need you."

Your heart sinks. You can tell from her tone of voice that this isn't an emergency—and, in fact, all she wants is to know where the scissors are. You've told her a thousand times not to interrupt you while you're on the phone. She never seems to remember. You've tried distracting her by gesturing for her to go watch TV, but she doesn't want to. You've excused yourself from the phone call and tried explaining why she shouldn't interrupt, only to hear the person on the other end grow impatient with your absence. In short, you've tried everything.

At least you think you have. Now try the "Two-Things-at-the-Same-Time" game and see if that works. You can play it at dinner, in the car, or standing in line. Kids love it.

If your child is a preschooler, begin by focusing on the words *same* and *different*. Make up any body motion and say, for example, "I'm tapping my head. Now I'm stamping my foot. Did I just do the *same* thing or something *different?*"

Then add the word *not*—that is, say, "I did tap my head. I did *not* _____?" Let your child fill in the blank, such as, "clap your hands." As long as your child shows interest, you can add things like, "I see a tree. Do you see the *same* thing or something *different?* What do you *not* see?" At the dinner table, you can say, "This is a salt shaker. This is a spoon. Are these the *same* thing or something *different?*" Young children, I've found, love to play with the word and pronounce it "deeferrrent."

Now you can say, "We're going to play the 'Two-Things-at-the-Same-Time' game. I can tap my head and stamp my foot *at the same time.* What can you do *at the same time?*" Children love to think of things like, "I can walk and chew gum at the same time," or, "I can sing and jump at the same time."

Now add, "I can *not* stand up and sit down at the *same* time. What can you *not* do at the *same* time?"

Four-year-old Philip held his nose and said, "I can *not* hold my nose and breathe at the same time."

And his eight-year-old sister said, "I can *not* do my homework and sleep at the same time," adding, "and I can *not* sing and drink water at the same time." These kids got so carried away listing the things they could *not* do at the same time that they made Mom and Dad play, too.

The next time Phil interrupted his mother on the phone, she simply asked, "Can I talk to you and on the phone *at the same time?*" Remembering the game, Phil smiled. Mom then added, "Can you think of something *different* to do while you wait?"

"I can go watch TV," Phil said.

---

The next time Phil interrupted his mother on the phone, she simply asked, "Can I talk to you and on the phone *at the same time?*" . . . "Can you think of something *different* to do while you wait?"

Of course, if his mom had suggested that, he probably would have refused. But now he doesn't have to resist the suggestion because he came up with it himself; if anything, he feels proud that he can think of something to do while he waits.

# 8

# Possessiveness

## When Kids Fight over Toys

"Gimme the truck. I had it first!"

"No, I did. It's mine."

"No, it's mine!"

"You never let me play!"

Every parent has heard children get into fights like this. Either they grab toys from one another, refuse to share, or dispute the amount of time that a toy needs to be shared. Sometimes they become so proprietary about a favorite toy that they refuse to share at all.

Typically, our impulse is to solve the dispute by being "fair"—that is, we try to ascertain who really had the truck first, how long he had it, and when would be the best time to share. But as most parents soon find out, the quest for fairness is often futile. The more you question your child about who had the truck first, or for how long he's been playing with it, the more he digs in and the angrier he becomes.

As for who had it first, you'll probably never know.

Sometimes, you're tempted to simply take the truck away, shouting, "If you two can't share the toy, neither of you will have it!"

Take a moment to think about what this strategy would accomplish. Taking the toy away does not guarantee that the kids will solve the problem. There is one thing it does guarantee: even if your children do comply in the moment and share the truck for now, nothing has happened to change how they feel inside, and how they will feel the next time they're faced with a situation like this.

What can you do instead? If you're the mother of the boy who grabbed the truck, you can ask one simple question: "What happened *after* you grabbed the toy?"

"He hit me," your son might say.

"If you two want to play with the same toy at the *same* time, what can you do to solve that problem?"

Asked this very question, four-year-old Brett said to his brother, "I'll roll the truck and you put the men inside." They both smiled; this was a satisfying solution.

Now you can say, "That's good thinking," or "You're a good problem solver." By avoiding comments as, "That's a good idea," you'll be praising your child not for *what* he thinks but *that* he thinks. If you praise a specific solution that your child comes up with, he might walk away feeling pleased that you like the idea, and think no further. A week later, when a similar problem recurs, he may offer the same solution—only to have the other child not agree to it. What then?

By formulating a new solution, your son can not only avoid a power play with you and a fight with his brother, but he is also more likely to get his own turn with the truck.

Is it ever OK not to share? While we all want our kids to be generous, a child who has what is to her a very precious toy, especially one that could break, or a toy so new that she wants to play with it on her own for a while, needs to be shown respect for her wants, too. To show your child you understand her feelings about this, you can ask, "Is there a reason you don't want your brother to play with your wagon?" Four-year-old Rudy said, "He might tear the wheels off." His mom replied, "OK. Is there something else you can share with your brother that will not break?" This kind of question shows a child we respect her feelings and is much less likely to end up in a power struggle and possible tears.

## Borrowing Without Permission: Parents to the Rescue?

Eleven-year-old Cindy comes home and sees Eve, her nine-year-old sister, wearing her sweater—again—after Cindy had asked Eve not to borrow

**Toy Wars**

Have you ever heard this common whine?:
"It's mine." *"No!* It's mine! It really is mine!"

And when this doesn't work, kids will shout till they burst:
"I had it first!" *"No!* I had it first."

You can take the toy away, so they'll no longer hit—
But that only makes the kids have a fit.

You can tell them to share so there will be no tears,
But that idea only falls on deaf ears.

You can explain now why they shouldn't fight:
"Someone will get hurt if you don't play right."

But they have heard this a thousand times before.
The thousandth-and-first time, they don't hear anymore.

Their fighting and screaming is driving you nuts—
Till you find yourself shouting, "No ifs, ands, or buts!"

When kids want to fight instead of to play,
Just ask them to think of a *different* way.

it. What happens next? Cindy shouts, "I told you not to go in my closet! Don't touch my stuff! Take it off right now! It's mine!" But Eve flashes her "make-me" look. That infuriates Cindy, who says, witheringly, "It looks ridiculous on you. It looks much better on me!"

"But I have a skirt to match," Eve says, not at all intimidated by her sister's fury, "and you don't."

The bickering goes on, each comment more venomous than the last.

Finally Cindy appeals to her mom, who tells her not to be so selfish. "But, Mom," Cindy begins, "I bought that sweater with my own money and . . ."

"That's enough," her mom says; she's heard it all before and is tired of dealing with the problem. "Figure it out yourself."

Cindy runs back to her sister and screams, "I wish you were never born!" At which point Eve rips the sweater off, throws it at Cindy, and says, "Your stuff doesn't fit me anyway. It's ugly. And you're too fat."

Cindy grabs the sweater and retreats to her room. But she is in tears. And so is Eve.

Kids this age fight over just about everything: shoes, shampoo, jewelry, CDs, videos. Some parents, like Cindy and Eve's, might just not want to deal with it. Others promise they'll solve the problem for their kids. When Dana complained that her sister keeps "borrowing" her jewelry, her mom assured her that she'd take care of this right away. A dad assured his son that he would talk to his brother about taking his bike without his permission. And another promised to get his daughter's CDs back for her. Mom and Dad to the rescue? Unfortunately, it's a shortsighted solution. Parents won't always be around to help solve disputes between siblings.

There are more foresightful ways of helping your kids when they're arguing over possessions:

- Bring your children together. Ask them to tell you what the problem is and what they can do to solve it.
- Ask them to think about whether their solution is or is not a good one, and why. If they decide it's not a good idea, ask them to think of an outcome that would make both of them happy.

When Cindy's mom reflected on her daughters' fight over the sweater, she approached Cindy and asked her what got her so angry.

"I hate that she just takes my things," Cindy said. "I wouldn't mind letting her borrow my clothes if she just asked first. I don't like to feel taken advantage of. I just want a little consideration. I'd do that for her."

Cindy's mom asked Cindy if she could think of a way she could let Eve know how she feels when Eve takes her things without permission. Cindy knocked on her sister's door, and when Eve opened it, Cindy said, "All you have to do is ask me first." Then she apologized for flying off the handle.

The girls ended up having a long talk together and eventually found themselves in Cindy's room where Cindy set aside three sweaters that Eve could borrow without permission. But if she wanted any of the others, she had to ask. Eve was delighted with this solution. Looking at her sister's happy face, Cindy realized that she really didn't mean what she said— and that she was glad that Eve was born after all. Smiling to herself, she thought, if she didn't have a sister, who would she trade clothes with?

As Cindy and Eve's mom learned, simply telling children to "figure it out" does not help them solve the problem. But rescuing children from the daily turmoil of life without involving them, as Dana's mom did when she "took care of" the problem of her sister borrowing her jewelry, isn't instructional either. That only relieves kids from having to think anymore about what's troubling them and why.

## When Preteens Stake Their Claim: "It's *My* Time!"

Mathew and Holly's parents just bought a new computer and put it in the family room for everyone to use. They did this not only because they couldn't afford to buy each child his or her own computer, but also because they wanted to monitor how much time their children spent online and with whom. This wouldn't be possible if the kids were squirreled away in their own rooms.

But as their dad told me, this wonderful new purchase caused more problems than it solved. As soon as they returned home from school, the kids raced to the computer: the first one to reach it took possession. That always turned out to be Mathew, who, at twelve, is three years older than his sister. Once he staked his claim to it, he stayed there for the rest of the afternoon, despite Holly's pleas for time.

One day, while going home on the school bus, Holly had a new idea. "I get dibs on the computer today," she said to Mathew. "OK?"

Mathew said, "We'll check with Mom."

"But I said it first!" Holly said.

Unnerved, Mathew said, "Mom's in charge. We'll have to ask her."

When they arrived home, Holly ran to the computer, making sure she was planted in front of it as if to stake her claim. Mathew knew there was no way of removing his sister without hurting her or doing something else he might regret. So he did the next best thing: he sought out his mom. "Holly claimed the computer on the bus coming home today," he said. "That's not fair. That's not how we decide who gets on it first."

"It's *my* time," Holly yelled in from the family room. "He can have it when I'm done."

Mom, who was caught in the middle, tried to negotiate an agreement so they could have equal time. She told Holly that she could have the computer until five o'clock, when it would be Mathew's turn. Holly unhappily agreed. However, when five o'clock rolled around, she realized that she'd spent all her time playing computer games and still needed the computer to do her homework. Agitated, she asked her mother for more time. Mathew, naturally, didn't think this was fair. So Mom negotiated a new compromise: Holly could use the computer till dinner and Mathew for the rest of the night.

"That's not fair!" Holly whined. "He'll have more time. And he only plays games on it. I use it for homework."

"Mathew needs the computer for work as much as you do," Mom said, raising her voice. She was tired of playing police officer. Holly agreed, but she was still mad.

That's when Dad arrived home. He listened to everyone's point of view, and then said, "We have a problem here. Can you think of a way to solve this?

After they calmed down, Mathew suggested, "Maybe we can take turns. Today it's me first, tomorrow it's you first." Holly didn't like that idea at all. Though Dad was tempted to just lay down the law, he took a deep breath and said, "I know you two can think of something. Think about it and let me know what you decide."

A few hours later, the kids came prancing into the living room with a brand-new idea. Mathew, the spokesperson, said, "We'll each do our homework first, and we'll toss a coin to see who gets first dibs."

Then Holly chimed in, "And maybe when we both finish our homework, we can play computer games together."

These days, Mathew and Holly enjoy the computer—both together and on their own.

If you're faced with this problem, you could solve it by buying a computer for each child. But if you can help your kids learn not to be so possessive, you might not have to purchase more than you really need. And think of the advantages of learning to live with one computer—your children could play together rather than gravitating to their own rooms, seeing their siblings only at dinner or on the school bus.

## "Get Out of My Space!"

Scott, nine, is playing with a friend when Tina, his younger sister, enters the bedroom they share. Feeling his space and his privacy are being intruded upon, he bosses his sister around. "Every time I'm playing with my friends, you have to bother us," he explodes. "Get out of here!"

"But it's my room, too," Tina explains.

"Yeah, but we were here first," answers Scott.

The conflict continues. "I'm just going to play by myself," Tina tries. "I won't bother you."

Unfazed, Scott replies, "You'll mess up everything. Just go away."

Does this kind of talk and lack of concern for each other sound familiar? If these were your kids, you might say, "Scott, your sister wants to play. She won't mess anything up. It's her room, too." But what would Scott think? Perhaps he doesn't care what his sister wants. And he might even conclude that his mom cares more about his sister's interests.

Here's another way you can help your kids solve this kind of problem. Ask each child, so the other can hear:

"How do you feel about the problem you're facing?"

"Can either of you think of a way to solve this problem so both of you will feel OK about it?"

When Tina was asked these questions, she said, "If I can come in now, you can come in when my friend Mia is here."

"OK," Scott replied, "but only if you don't bug us."

It doesn't matter what specific solution the siblings settle on—whether to share the space or schedule use of the room. What *does* matter is that one child has come up with a solution the other can accept.

Sometimes even when children have their own bedrooms, one still ends up feeling intruded upon. Eleven-year-old Max, for example, has a room all to himself, and his prized miniature car collection sits proudly displayed on his dresser. His brother, Evan, who is seven, constantly wants to come into Max's room to play with the cars. "You're going to break them!" Max yells. "And don't come in here without permission!"

Evan leaves—only to return a few minutes later while Max is getting a snack. When Max returns, he finds his brother sitting on his bed playing with a toy he brought in from his own room. "What are you doing in here!" yells Max. "This is *my* room! *Get out of my space!*" Evan, totally dejected, leaves.

Mom and Dad hear the screaming and don't want to see Evan so upset. They know that explaining to Max how he's making Evan feel will not change the way Max talks to his brother when he's so angry. They also know that suggesting to Evan that he play with his own toys in his own room will not make him feel better or address the main issue—that Evan really wants to play in his brother's room.

Here's how Dad talked about the situation to his boys:

**Dad:** Max, what's the problem?

**Max:** Evan keeps coming in my room. He messes everything up and he's going to break my cars. I hate it when I walk into my room and there he is.

**Evan:** But he never plays with me.

**Dad:** Evan, is the problem that he never plays with you or that you want to play in his room?

**Evan:** I want him to play with me. I wasn't bothering his cars.

**Dad:** Max, when Evan goes into your room when you're not there, how do you feel about that?

**Max:** Mad.

**Dad:** How do you think Evan feels when you yell at him like that?

**Max:** Sad.

**Dad:** Max, is it that you never want him in your room or that you don't want him to go in there without asking first?

**Max:** I hate it when he just comes in my room and I'm not there, or barges in when I'm doing my homework.

**Dad:** OK. What can you say to Evan so he'll know what you really want?

**Max:** Please ask me and then I can decide if I want to let you in my room.

**Dad:** And Evan, can you think of a *different* way to get Max to play with you that won't make him feel so mad?

**Evan:** Max, can we play checkers tonight? Just for a little while?

**Max:** OK, but just for a little while. I have a lot of homework tonight.

It didn't matter where they played—in Max's room or on the dining room table. What really mattered was that Evan learned to respect his older brother's need for his own space and for privacy. In time, Evan recognized that his brother would play with him—and sometimes, he'd even invite him into his room.

# 9

# Defiance, Tattling, and Lying

## "Why Is My Child So Defiant?"

Does your child resist your requests, suggestions, or even explanations about his well-being? What do you do? What do you say? Does his defiance get so out of control that you just give up?

Three-year-old Elizabeth was at the stage during which she tested her parents at every turn. When her mother would say, "It's nap time," Elizabeth would defiantly scream, "*No!* I'm not tired!"

"If you don't take your nap now," her mother warned, having been through this every day for the past month, "you won't have your TV time tonight."

"I don't care!" Elizabeth answered.

Her mother took a deep breath and tried a somewhat more positive approach.

"Do I say no every time you ask me to do something? Did I say no when you wanted your milk and cookies? Did I say no when you wanted to go to the zoo?" She paused, noting that Elizabeth didn't seem to be paying any attention. Valiantly, she tried again: "I'm asking you to nap for your own good. If you don't, you'll be too tired to play with Daddy when he gets home."

Elizabeth just shrugged. She refused to nap and, as her mother predicted, fell asleep on the couch five minutes before her father came home. She woke up cranky just as dinner was ending.

That night, while bathing Elizabeth, her mother had an idea. "What happened tonight when Daddy came home?"

For the first time all day, Elizabeth looked sad. She always enjoyed greeting her dad when he came home and looked forward all day to playing with him.

"I didn't see Daddy," Elizabeth said.

"What can you do tomorrow so you won't miss Dad when he comes home?" Mom asked.

"I can take a nap," Elizabeth said. Her mother reminded her of this conversation the next day after lunch. Elizabeth remembered and climbed into her bed with her favorite stuffed bear and slept for an hour. That night, she was wide awake when her father came home.

Elizabeth's mother helped her daughter to think about consequences. But there are other ways to use the problem-solving approach. Mark, age ten, refused to take showers. His mother tried demanding that he shower each night. When that didn't work, she tried what she thought was a positive approach. "You know," she said during a calm moment, "if you don't shower, you're more likely to get sick because of all the germs on your skin. Also, when you don't shower, your body starts to smell. You won't have many friends. No one will want to be around you."

But the more Mom explained, the more Mark resisted. And when he did, Mom became even more exasperated and bewildered. What kind of a child doesn't listen to reason?

I wasn't surprised when I heard that demanding and explaining didn't work. Those two approaches rarely do. What Mom needed to do was stop talking and explaining and let Mark get a word in edgewise. One afternoon, driving home from the library, Mom asked, in a deliberately neutral voice, "What bothers you about taking showers?"

And then something interesting happened. She learned something she didn't know. "I don't like to shower," Mark said, "'cause showers aren't fun."

"Well, I have to go to work each day and that isn't fun," his mother started to say. But then she stopped herself. She decided to use the problem-solving approach. "What can you do to make it fun?" she asked instead.

Mark thought for a moment. "Well, I guess I can pretend that I'm standing under a waterfall in Hawaii."

That night, Mark took a shower right before bed. He seemed surprisingly enthusiastic about it. But maybe it's not really that surprising. Mark was excited because he'd come up with his own reason to take a shower. Had his mother suggested that he think of the Hawaiian waterfall, he probably would have shrugged her off.

We don't always have to tell our kids what to do, or even why to do it. Very often, they know. Sometimes all we have to do is encourage them to think about it. And if we ask them, they'll tell us.

---

We don't always have to tell our kids what to do, or even why to do it. Very often, they know.

---

## "Stop That Sassy Talk!"

You've just finished a pleasant family dinner. "Annie, please take the dishes to the sink," you say. Annie's nine, and she's been helping with the dirty dishes for the past two years. It's one of her favorite household chores— at least until recently. Lately, when you ask her to do this or any other simple request, she either procrastinates, defies you by saying, "No!" or "Not now!," or else rolls her eyes and gives you that "You-can't-make-me" look. Tonight, she simply ignores your request and begins to walk upstairs. When Dad tells her to come back and finish her chores, she tauntingly murmurs, "No, thank you."

Frustrated, Dad turns to you and asks, "Will you please talk to your daughter?"

"Just calm down," you say soothingly. "Leave the dishes on the table. I'll make sure she does them in a few minutes."

But that doesn't satisfy Dad. "Annie!" he yells. "Come down here this instant and finish your chores! If you don't, you'll be grounded!"

Does this "power discipline"—demands, commands, and threats— make Annie any less defiant?

Joanna, eight, began blowing on a whistle and wouldn't stop. The noise became louder and louder until her mother couldn't stand it. "Please stop!" her mother shouted.

Joanna didn't stop. "It's hurting my ears," her mother explained.

Joanna kept blowing. "Joanna," her mother said again. "I explained why I want you to stop. Now please put the whistle down."

Joanna put her hand on her waist, stared her mother right in the eyes, and said, "What are you going to do about it?"

"Don't use that tone of voice with me, young lady! I *never* talked to my mother like that! Just wait till your father gets home!" Joanna didn't pay attention to any of this. Exasperated, her mom groaned, "Am I talking to a brick wall!?"

In her book *Momisms: What She Says and What She Really Means*, Cathy Hamilton humorously reminds us how our parents used these and other gems of wisdom to, among other things, "cajole, shame, inspire, threaten . . . and bewilder" us. But such "momisms," in addition to shaming and threatening kids, also belittle them. And pity the poor father who eagerly anticipates a big welcome when he comes home from a hard day's work but instead has to face a child who has been warned, "Wait till your father comes home."

How can you use the problem-solving approach to respond to your child's defiance, sassy tone, and annoying back talk?

I suggest that you ask this series of questions:

"How do you think we feel when you talk to us like that?"
"How do you feel knowing how we feel about what you're saying?"
"Can you think of a different way to talk to us so we all won't feel bad [sad, disappointed, etc.]?"

By asking instead of telling our kids how we feel, they begin to consider how their behavior affects other people. Asking them to describe their true emotions helps them *experience* those feelings, not just mouth them.

When Joanna's mother asked Joanna if she could come up with a different way to talk to her, the question took Joanna by surprise. She looked at her mom and smirked. But then, after a long pause, she said, "OK, Mom, I won't blow that whistle anymore."

If Joanna continued to blow the whistle, her mother could, for her own sanity, simply take it away. She could even let her daughter know how angry she feels. In my view, parents can say that they're angry when they feel it. It would be unnatural not to; in addition, anger is an emotion kids have to learn to cope with. But even while the whistle is out of reach, Mom can still talk to Joanna using the problem-solving approach to encourage her daughter to become considerate of others.

It took time for Annie and Joanna to change their behavior. But just as we ask our kids to think of a different way to talk to us when they whine, make demands, or tune us out, we can ask ourselves to think of different ways to talk to our kids—rather than resorting to "Don't use that tone of voice with me!"; "Wait till your father gets home!"; or "Am I talking to a brick wall?!"

## Dawdling: Defiance or Distraction?

"Not now."

"In a minute."

"Later."

Many children resort to these words more frequently than they realize. "My kids never do anything when I ask them to," parents complain. "They dawdle, whether it's time to get ready for school or to go to dinner at Grandma's house."

Does this scene sound familiar? It's seven thirty in the morning and your child, who should be eating her breakfast, is just getting up to brush her teeth. You'll have to rush like crazy to get to the school bus on time. You're stressed and exasperated. And you *know* she's dragging her heels just to annoy you.

"If you're not ready in five minutes," you say, your patience running out, "I'm leaving the house without you." But what good will that do?

Many parents naturally assume that their children's lack of responsiveness means that they're being defiant or willfully oppositional. Are delaying tactics always an example of testing the limits? Are children always trying to control the situation? Do they purposely push your hot button? Are their behaviors always what they seem to be?

Maybe not. Your children may not be actively defying you but instead are distracted—by the television, their brother, a phone call—or suffering from a lack of focus. It is also possible that they are unaware of, or unconcerned about, time and the need to keep to a schedule. Telling a five-year-old, for example, that he has five minutes to finish dressing has no real meaning for him—and even if it did, he wouldn't interpret the remark with as much urgency.

Remember, too, that very young children need lots of extra time to slip into their pants, adjust their socks, and tie their shoelaces. They're not dawdling: they're mastering new skills. If you rush them, they'll stop feeling pride in their very real accomplishments.

If your older child dawdles and procrastinates while getting ready for school, you can help by providing some much-needed structure. Agree upon a time each day during which you'll help your child prepare for the next day at school. And make sure that you leave *yourself* ample time to do that. Ask him:

"What do you need in your backpack for tomorrow?"
"Where are your pencils and notebooks? Where is your calculator?"
"Do you need your gym shorts or your clarinet?"

Here's how one mom helped her eight-year-old son devise a solution to his procrastination problem. At the beginning of each week, they make a morning checklist of what he needs to bring on different days—such as library books on Tuesdays, speech notebook on Mondays and Wednesdays. The list also includes the dates that special projects are due, as well as daily tasks like getting dressed and brushing teeth. "My son loves to check off each thing for each day, and it keeps him focused on what he needs to do next without me or my nanny nagging him," his mom told me. She had the feeling that had she not involved him in creating the list, he would have refused to try it. And she's probably right.

You can also get your child more actively involved by involving him in preparatory tasks ahead of time. For example, you can:

• Go shopping together and let him pick out his own backpack.

- Ask your child what he wants for lunch.
- Involve him in making the sandwich and packing lunch.
- Let him select his clothes for the next day the night before—and don't grit your teeth if you don't approve.

If your child *still* dawdles, ask a series of questions:

"What might happen if you take so long to get dressed?"
"How will you feel if you're late to school?"
"What can you do tonight so that you won't be late tomorrow morning?"

In conversation, I've learned that many kids who dawdle in the morning really do worry about missing the school bus. They just haven't realized that delaying getting dressed could be a cause. You can help guide them toward this realization by asking, "What might happen if the school bus comes to pick you up and you're not there?"

If, however, your child is dawdling because he doesn't want to go to school, talk to him about why he feels this way. In this case, the problem isn't dawdling; it's his solution to the problem he's having with school.

When you encourage your child to think about what she's doing, involve her in the process of planning ahead, and allow enough time to do what she has to do, you'll both feel a lot less stress. She'll enjoy the day more, and you will, too.

## Help Your Child Stop Tattling

You may not notice the pattern for a few days. But gradually you start realizing that when your eight-year-old comes home from school, she's full of stories about who did what to whom. You start listening more closely when she explains that she has been telling the teacher what goes on behind her back. You also notice that your child isn't getting called for as many playdates as she used to.

That's when you realize that she may be turning into a tattletale. Worse, the kids in her class are starting to notice.

You tell her to stop or she won't have any friends and that no one will trust her. She doesn't seem to hear you. You explain that if she tattles on others, they will start tattling on her. She doesn't hear that, either. What can you do?

Jan, nine, thought her teacher would like her better if she informed her about her classmates' activities. She told the teacher, for instance, that Faye tore up Adrienne's math sheet. As a result, Faye had to stay inside during recess. Jan felt special. But Faye wouldn't talk to her after class, and she let Jan know how she felt about this.

Jan's mom talked with her daughter about this the problem-solving way:

**Mom:** What happened when you told the teacher what Faye did?
**Jan:** Faye got really mad. She told me she won't ever be my friend now.
**Mom:** How do you feel about that?
**Jan:** Sad.
**Mom:** What can you do next time you feel like tattling so that won't happen and you won't feel that way?
**Jan:** Just stay out of it.

Children who can explore what they're doing and why will easily graduate to thinking about how other kids feel. From this realization, it's an easy step for them to figure out how to act differently next time.

If your child consistently tattles, perhaps she feels, as Jan did, that her teacher doesn't really like her. Maybe the teacher yelled at her, or spoke to her harshly. Using the problem-solving approach, you can ask your child what happened before the teacher yelled at her. Your child could have been talking during a lesson, or disobeyed a request. If so, she may have tattled in order to "atone" for her mistake and to get back in the good graces of her teacher.

"Mom, Billy got in trouble in school today 'cause he called the other kids a bad name," said seven-year-old Carrie the moment she returned from school. Carrie's mother wasn't sure whether to punish her son for name-calling, thank Carrie for letting her know, or both. The next day, Carrie came home with another story about her brother.

This gave her mother pause. Why was Carrie feeling the need to tattle? She then realized that she'd been very preoccupied lately with some difficulties at work and that it was likely that Carrie was vying for her attention.

However, if she began giving Carrie her full attention, Carrie might interpret it as a reward for tattling. Instead, she asked Carrie to think about how her brother would feel if he knew she told her he called kids names at school, and what might happen if he ever found out about her tattling.

"He'd be mad," Carrie said.

"Can you think of a *different* way to get my attention?" her mother asked.

Carrie thought for a moment, smiled, and said, "Mom, I drew a picture in school today. Do you want to see it?" Carrie was learning to become more sensitive to both her brother's needs and her own.

An older child who sees a younger sibling playing near a hot oven needs to let his mother know right away. A child who witnesses someone being beaten up or hears a credible threat needs to notify someone in authority immediately. A child who sees a bully get away with bullying behavior day after day needs to share this information with teachers or administrators.

You can help your child distinguish between tattling and protecting by asking some questions during a quiet moment:

"Why might you want to tell someone what someone is doing?"
"Will someone really get hurt?"
"Will it really help things if you tell?"
"If no one will really get hurt, what might happen next if you *do* snitch?"
"Can you think of something else to do, instead of snitching, that would solve the problem?"

At the same time you discourage tattling, you can help your child understand when it's important to share information with adults. Informing adults that someone is in genuine and/or imminent danger isn't snitching, it's being responsible.

# "You're Lying!"

Running through the living room, your ten-year-old broke your favorite flowerpot. "It wasn't me!" he cries, blaming his brother.

Your eight-year-old threw a ball that broke a window in your house. "I didn't do it!" he maintains—"it was another kid."

Your four-year-old spilled juice on the floor, and proclaims, "Johnny did it."

Your child sounds sincere—but you know she's lying. You try berating her: "Don't you know right from wrong by now!" But that doesn't help. You've tried to explain the virtues of telling the truth, and how lying only makes a bad situation worse. But in the end, all your words fell on deaf ears. You've tried punishing him for lying, but that only seemed to make him more dishonest. He began lying just to stay out of trouble.

No one learns to tell the truth by being yelled at. Here's a different way of talking with your child about the importance of honesty. If you know, for example, that your child is blaming another, ask:

"How do you think I feel when you blame your brother?"
"How do you think your brother feels?"
"What can you do so your brother and I won't feel that way?"

Then shift to the end result of the accident or misdeed: the broken flowerpot, the broken window, or the spilled juice. Ask, for example:

"What might happen if the juice is on the floor?"
"How would you feel if that happened?"
"What can you do so that won't happen?"

Pam, four, accidentally spilled juice on the floor and quickly blamed her brother. After she was helped to think about people's feelings and to recognize that telling the truth was more important than upsetting her brother, her mom tried to focus her daughter's attention on what to do next. "What might happen if the juice stays on the floor?" Pam didn't answer at first. So Mom gave her a hint, without directly answering the question, by asking, "What might happen if someone didn't see the juice and kept walking?"

Now Pam understood that someone might fall and get hurt. When asked how she would feel if that happened, Pam said, "Sad."

"What can you do so that won't happen?" her mom asked.

Pam got a paper towel and wiped up the spill.

If you know that your child broke something, or did anything that he wants to deny, don't focus on the act itself. The spilled juice is history. The broken flowerpot is history. You can't put it back together and you can't change what happened—but you *can* change how you talk about it after the fact, as Pam's mother did.

Instead of focusing on "Who did it?" focus on "What can you do now?" When asked this question, the boy who broke the flowerpot decided to save money from his allowance to buy his mother a new pot, and the boy who broke the window promised not to play ball near the house anymore. Both boys no longer had a need to blame someone else. They felt safe to tell the truth.

Children need to feel safe before they are comfortable telling the truth. If your child fears that she'll be yelled at, she'll be too afraid to take the risk that honesty requires. As a twelve-year-old explained to me, "I'm not afraid to tell the truth because I know my parents won't hurt me."

Isn't that what you really want for your child?

## 10

# Physical Aggression, Bullies, and Victims

### "Mommy, Tommy Hit Me!"

Has your child ever come home from school whining, "Mommy, Tommy hit me"? Here's how one mom talked to her young son about this.

**Mom:** Hit him back.
**Kevin:** But I'm afraid.
**Mom:** I don't want you to be so timid.
**Kevin:** OK.

Another mom took a different tack:

**Mom:** Don't hit him back, tell the teacher instead.
**Danny:** But they'll call me a tattletale.
**Mom:** If you don't tell the teacher, he'll keep on hitting you.

The advice may sound very different, but in fact both mothers used the same approach—they both did the thinking for their children. Neither child had to consider what to do—only how to do it.

Here's how Kevin's mom handled the same situation after learning the problem-solving approach.

**Mom:** What happened *before* he hit you?
**Kevin:** I called him stupid.

**Mom:** Was something bothering you?

**Kevin:** He tore up my book.

**Mom:** How did you feel when he tore up your book?

**Kevin:** Mad.

**Mom:** And how do you think he felt when you called him stupid?

**Kevin:** Mad.

**Mom:** Can you think of something *different* to do so he won't hit you and you both won't be mad?

**Kevin:** I could tear his book.

**Mom:** And what might happen then?

**Kevin:** We'll fight.

**Mom:** Do you want that to happen?

**Kevin:** No.

**Mom:** Can you think of something *different* to do so that won't happen?

**Kevin:** I could tell him I won't be his friend.

**Mom:** That's a *different* way. Good thinking.

In this scenario, Kevin's mom didn't tell Kevin—who was only four years old—what to do. Instead, she helped her son think. And she rewarded him for the *way* he thought about his problem rather than the specific solution or the problem's outcome. The more Kevin practices his problem-solving skills, the more likely it is he will use them the next time he comes up against a difficult situation.

In addition, by encouraging him to pay attention to his feelings, and Tommy's feelings, Kevin's mother is fostering empathy, a quality that will help him develop good relationships in the future. Kevin will get in the habit of treating people well because he wants to, not because he fears punishment.

## When Your Child Hurts Others

Your five-year-old hits a friend who refuses to share a toy.

Your four-year-old kicks his sister when she changes the channel on the television to the show she wants to watch.

Your three-year-old bites and screams when she doesn't get her way.

You try telling your child to "be nice," but the problem is that when children are angry, they don't *feel* nice.

You try to explain to your child that she's hurting other people, but when she's angry, she doesn't care about anyone else.

Now you're exasperated. What can you do? You can punish him. That may stop him from hitting or kicking, but it won't change how your child feels inside. You may feel like simply giving up. But that won't help him learn to change how he reacts to frustration or anger.

Helping your child learn to redirect aggression is important—and the sooner he learns, the better. Research shows that aggression that shows up when children are young doesn't go away on its own and could, depending on its frequency and intensity, be a warning sign that your child will encounter problems later on in school.

Instead of explaining, yelling, punishing, or walking away, try the following.

Ask your child: "How do you think your friend feels when you hit him? How do you think your sister feels when you kick her?"

Your child may say something like, "She feels angry."

Then ask, "What might your friend [or sister] say or do next?"

Your child may say, "Hit me back."

Then ask, "Do you want that to happen?"

If your child acknowledges that he doesn't really want things like that to happen—and most children don't—ask, "Can you think of something *different* to do so that won't happen?"

You'll be surprised to hear what she may come up with.

In a moment of rage, three-year-old Lucy bit her father. Just as he was about to spank her and send her to her room, her mom asked, "Can you think of a *different* way to tell your father how you feel?" Lucy paused, looked at her father, and hugged him. Her gesture took everyone by surprise. Just think how long both father and daughter might have remained enraged had Lucy's mother not asked that simple question.

Older children can learn to curb this kind of aggression, too. Henry, a fifth-grader, was easily angered when a classmate bothered him. After participating in a service-learning project at school, which included the problem-solving approach to help children learn to make others feel good, Henry wrote letters to kids in a hospital and decorated baskets for them. This, in combination with talking about people's feelings when he bullied them, helped Henry care more about others. He told me, "When I heard about how happy the kids in the hospital were, it made me feel grown up. I feel different about myself. I think about others, not just myself." As Curry Bailey, director of this service-learning project in the Philadelphia Public Schools and coordinator of the Middle School Drug Prevention and Safety Program, said, "Many children who behave as bullies really do have empathy. They just have to learn to show it." Henry, I believe, has shown us how.

While Bailey was referring to children Henry's age, the problem-solving approach can also help much younger children think about what they really do and do not want to happen in light of how they and others may feel. With encouragement from Mom and Dad, they too will be able to consider what they can do and why.

## It's Not Always Time for a Time-Out

Are you a fan of "time-out" as a way of guiding your kids to do what you want? Many people are. But have you ever asked yourself what a time-out really teaches children?

If a time-out is used as a genuine calming-down period, it can be a big help. After everyone calms down, it's often easier to talk about the incidents leading up to the confrontation and sift through the threads of who did what to whom.

But a time-out can be abused. This happens when it's administered in front of others. That can prove especially humiliating. In these circumstances, the period during which the child is isolated is a time when anger and frustration build up, often to the boiling point.

Time-outs are also misused when they are administered before parents understand the scope of the problem. Five-year-old Austin's mother sent him to a time-out when he refused to help clear the table after dinner. She thought he was just being defiant. One day, before sending him for yet another time-out, she asked him why he didn't want to help with the dishes. "'Cause they'll fall and break," he said. With that, Austin's mom realized that he wasn't resisting doing chores; rather, he was afraid of doing this one specific chore. When she asked Austin how he'd like to help around the house, he suggested that he help her fold laundry. Austin's mother realized that she had used the time-out prematurely, resorting to it before she knew the true source of her son's resistance.

Sometimes time-outs are used—ineffectively—as punishment. For example, when David and Sam got into a tug-of-war over a truck, their mother would usually send them both to a time-out chair—hoping they would calm down. Instead, one usually screamed and the other cried, "I don't want to go to time-out!" The problem with time-out in this case is that it separates the boys from the toy, from the problem to be solved, and from each other. If they're thinking about anything at all, it's probably how to get back at each other, or at Mom. The time apart does nothing to change how either child is feeling inside. If anything, it makes both boys feel worse. They have time to kindle their own hurt feelings, not to figure out how to solve the problem.

After David and Sam's mom learned the problem-solving approach, she handled the same problem by asking each child how he felt, and if he could think of a different way to solve the problem. David looked at Sam, paused, and then said, "You can have the truck first, but when it's my turn I'll tell you and you have to give it back."

Sam was satisfied with that solution. David gave the truck to his brother, they both smiled, and that was the end of that. There were no power plays, no screaming, and no thoughts of "revenge" building up inside. It proved a very workable solution—and an especially creative one, given the fact that the children were so young: David was only five, and Sam, three.

Like other tools, time-outs work—but only when they're used appropriately, as a method of cooling down when tempers flare. It's not a substitute for good communication or for learning how to problem-solve.

Children learn more about themselves and others when they talk things out and resolve issues for themselves.

# To Spank or Not to Spank

In the middle of a "did not, did so" argument with his younger brother, five-year-old Ivan suddenly swats the younger child across his face.

Squirming at the curb, waiting for the light to change green, six-year-old Becky suddenly lets go of her mother's hand and runs out into the heavily trafficked street.

What would you do?

Your first impulse, and that of many parents, may be to spank your child. Some parents follow through; others refrain. What's best?

When I ask parents why they spank their kids, many tell me, "It works." When I ask what they mean by that, some reply, "He stops hitting his brother," or, "She won't run out into the street ever again."

Based on an extensive review of this subject, Columbia University researcher Elizabeth Gershoff reports that 94 percent of U.S. parents—a surprisingly high number—spank their kids by the age of three or four, with "spanking" defined as anything from light smacks to harsh beatings, and this finding is corroborated by psychologist Murray Straus. Gershoff concludes that spanking probably does stop a particular behavior from taking place in the moment. If you rely on frequent, harsh spankings, you may be surprised to learn what else Gershoff discovered:

- Spanking is a form of overpowering a child. When children feel powerless, they not only react with anger and frustration but may also feel the need to regain that power by exercising it on people whom they perceive as less threatening—namely, other kids at school. That's how bullies are born. Bullying is about regaining lost power.
- In an attempt to avoid being spanked, some children avoid their parents, at least emotionally. That leads them to trust their parents less, which means that children won't believe the very values that parents are trying to instill.
- Spanking is not an educational tool in that it doesn't teach children why hitting is mean or why running into a crowded street without looking can be dangerous. Often, children who are spanked react by

finding a way to do what they want without getting caught—or acting impulsively without thinking of potential dangers.

• Because spanking works by inflicting hurt on another person, children can perceive that spanking is an acceptable way to vent anger. They can think, "If Mom or Dad can hurt me, it's OK for me to hurt someone when I'm mad." In this way, using spanking teaches the very behavior it is attempting to stamp out.

There is another unintended consequence of spanking that I learned about when I asked a four-year-old boy why he grabbed a truck from a classmate. The boy replied, "He hit me, but I don't care. I got the truck."

This is a chilling statement, because it may be true that the boy really didn't care that he got hit. If kids are often spanked at home and hit at school, they can become immune to the pain—that is, they learn to endure the momentary hurt so that they can get what they want. If children become impervious to this form of discipline, we've lost control of them. They may not care what we do anymore.

People often ask me for my opinion on spanking. I don't say, "Never spank." An occasional spanking won't hurt your child, and it may legitimately relieve your own anger and frustration. However, if you rely on spanking, you'll encounter many unintended consequences. Perhaps the most serious result is that it teaches your child to disregard his own feelings. Learning to care about one's own feelings is the first step toward developing empathy for others.

Bonnie Aberson, who works with families, told me that one father, who had genuinely believed that spanking was the best way to stop his son from hurting his brother, had a real change of heart after learning problem-solving alternatives. "I used to use power, but I felt powerless," he explained. This father and his son have learned to use words instead of their hands.

If you resort to physical force, your child may end up fearing and distrusting you, and potentially even avoiding you—just the opposite of what you want to happen.

# 11

# Emotional Aggression

## When Preschoolers Hurt Others

Rachel and Tammy, two four-year-olds in preschool, played together often, but lately Rachel had become very bossy. When Tammy wouldn't be
"the baby" in the doll corner, Rachel threatened, "If you don't be the baby,
I won't be your friend!" When Tammy still wouldn't do what Rachel asked,
Rachel added, "I won't invite you to my birthday party." When Tammy
was still unmoved, Rachel thought of a way to really hurt her friend. She
went to the kids already playing in the doll corner and told them not to
let Tammy in.

Tammy, now very upset, told the teacher that the kids wouldn't let her
into the doll corner, but didn't know why, until one of them spilled the
beans, reporting it was Rachel who told them to keep her out.

The teacher, wanting to nip this very hurtful kind of behavior in the
bud, informed Rachel's mother, who was stunned. Rachel had never done
anything like this before, at least to her knowledge. When her mother
asked why she did that, Rachel said she didn't know. And with such a
general question, Rachel probably was, in fact, unaware of what made
her want to hurt her friend like that. Her mom explained how bad her
behavior made her friend feel, but Rachel didn't seem to care. Now, very
concerned, Rachel's mom, who learned the problem-solving way of talking with her child, asked her very specific and concrete questions to help
her think more about how what she did would affect not only her friend,
but herself.

**Mom:** Rachel, did Tammy do something in school today that made you feel angry?

**Rachel:** I told her to "be the baby and I'll be the mommy" and she didn't want to play with me.

**Mom:** And how did you feel about that?

**Rachel:** Mad.

**Mom:** What else did she say?

**Rachel:** I'm not a baby.

**Mom:** Do you think she didn't want to play with you, or that she didn't want to be the baby?

**Rachel:** I don't know.

**Mom:** You were so angry, you really wanted to hurt her. What did you do next?

**Rachel:** I don't know.

**Mom:** *(helping her remember, in a nonthreatening tone of voice)* What did you say to the kids in the dollhouse?

**Rachel:** I told them not to let her in.

**Mom:** How do you think Tammy felt then?

**Rachel:** Mad.

**Mom:** Did you really want to hurt her so much?

**Rachel:** Yes!

**Mom:** *(recognizing her anger might have been in the heat of the moment)* What might happen if you hurt your friends like that?

**Rachel:** They won't play with me.

**Mom:** Do you really want that to happen?

**Rachel:** No.

**Mom:** If Tammy didn't want to be the baby, how could you find out what she did want to do?

**Rachel:** I could ask her.

**Mom:** Good thinking. You're a good problem solver.

Rachel may not have been able to stop her bossy behavior in one day, but this kind of dialogue provides an important start. First, Rachel's mom helped her identify the real problem, that Tammy may just not have wanted to be the "baby"—not that she didn't want to play with her. But most important, Rachel's mom knew that if she continued to talk to her daughter the problem-solving way, she could nip behaviors in the bud that might cause her to be rejected by her peers later on.

## "Peter's Picking on Me!"—How to Help When Your Child Is Teased

Ten-year-old Terry was whining because Peter, a classmate, kept calling him names. Terry's dad told him to ignore Peter, walk away, or tell the teacher. Taking this advice, Terry ignored Peter's most recent taunting and walked away, but later complained that he still felt sad, frustrated, and angry. He also worried that if he told the teacher, other kids would find out and try to get revenge, which would hurt him even more.

Terry's father doesn't know what to suggest now but believes he has to come up with a solution. It would be more helpful if he could help Terry learn to think of his own solutions. To foster his problem-solving skills, he can ask Terry the following questions:

> "Why do you think Peter needs to pick on you?"
> "Is there another reason?"
> "How do you think he might be feeling inside?"
> "How do you feel when someone teases you?"
> "What can you do or say when someone does that?"

Questions like these focus children's attention on feelings—their own, and the feelings of others. This helps them to realize that relationships are reciprocal, and that they should treat others as they wish to be treated. They also come to realize that people act as they do for many different reasons.

Ten-year-old Marc, for instance, was mad at Jon, his classmate, who always teased Marc about his braces. After a problem-solving discussion with his father, Marc began to wonder *why* Jon acted the way he did. One day he noticed that Jon never looked happy. The next time they found themselves together on the playground, Marc asked Jon what was wrong. "I can't believe my parents are divorced," Jon said quietly. "I'm so used to them both being around. Now Mom found someone else she likes and I don't like him much." This revelation helped Marc feel differently about Jon. The next time Jon called him a name, Marc disarmed him by saying, "Let's be friends. I'll teach you how to shoot baskets." Today, these boys are best friends.

There are other solutions to problems like this, and children can come up with their own once they learn the skill of problem solving. Ten-year-old Lisa, for example, was constantly called "Too-tall" because she was so tall and skinny. After her mother asked her, "What can you do so the other girls won't hurt you?" Lisa thought hard about it. Feeling too timid to confront the kids directly, she decided to write a letter to the ringleader of the kids who were teasing her. In this letter, she explained how she felt. "They were so surprised they stopped teasing me," she happily reports.

Joey, who was also ten, grew upset every time one of his classmates called him "Bacon" because of his weight. Joey knew how to think the problem-solving way, and tried to come up with his own solution. Cleverly, he relied on his sense of humor. One afternoon when the boys started calling him "Bacon," he paused, looked directly into their eyes, and with a slight smile said, "Yeah, and I sizzle. I sizzle." The kids laughed and never called him Bacon again. Today, four years later, Joey is very popular and doing very well in school.

When Terry's dad helped him think about what he could do or say when Peter teased him, Terry also came up with a unique idea on his own. The next time Peter called him a name as they were leaving school, Terry took out a piece of bubble gum and began chewing. When Peter asked for a piece, Terry said, "No, 'cause you called me a name." Terry no longer appeared weak, and that was the last time Peter teased Terry.

Leonard, a fifth-grader, found a way to deal with his problem without appearing weak, either. After being continuously teased for wearing "silly-looking glasses," he won an essay-writing contest, which gained him the newfound respect of his classmates. "You know," he told them, in a friendly tone of voice, "I couldn't have seen what I wrote without these glasses."

If your child is being teased, try to help him focus on his strengths: perhaps he excels at sports, or chess, or has a flair for drama. By thinking about what he does well, he will come to feel good about himself. And this feeling is often contagious—once your child feels better about his own abilities, his classmates may notice his new demeanor and come to see him in a new light.

With your help, children can learn to modify their behavior, like sharing and taking turns. They can also learn to change how they respond to others who tease them about things over which they have no control, like their looks. To give them the skills to accomplish this, brainstorm with your child; come up with a list of possible retorts your child can use the next time he's teased. Some kids take a humorous approach: "I may be fat on Earth, but people on other planets find me very handsome." Other children may respond more seriously: "You think I'm too skinny, but it's just that we have different builds. Everyone does."

In all these situations, children turned their negative experiences into positive ones. Things would have turned out very differently for them if they followed conventional advice and ignored those who teased them, walked away, or told the teacher.

Why is it so important for children to have skills to defuse being teased? If left unattended, emotional scars can last for life. Ben, now age twenty, was a scrawny teenager with long legs and short arms. He was constantly called "dork" and "nerd" at school. Although he grew into a very handsome and popular young man, he still perceives himself as "ugly" and has difficulty forming friendships and sustaining romantic relationships. Had Ben been able to end his role of the victim when he was younger, he may have grown up not just to *be* popular but to *feel* popular.

## When Friends Betray Each Other's Secrets

Has your child ever come home upset because one of her friends betrayed her trust and revealed something your child told her in confidence?

Ten-year-old Cara felt hurt because her best friend, Suzanne, told another girl that Cara had a crush on an older guy at school. Situations like this are not uncommon in the life of a preteen. And broken trust can be more painful and more lasting than a punch in the nose. Cara not only thought she lost her best friend, she also felt betrayed—that someone she cared about didn't really care about her.

You could try to comfort a child in Cara's predicament by saying, "Tell her you're hurt that she broke your trust." Or you could say, "If you're afraid to tell her how you feel, get a friend to tell her." You might even find yourself saying, "If you don't tell her how you feel, she'll keep doing things like that."

While all this is good advice, you are still doing the thinking for your child. Try talking with your preteen about this in another way—a problem-solving way. Here's how Cara's mom helped her daughter think more about her own feelings and why her friend might have betrayed her trust.

**Mom:** How did you feel when Suzanne told your secret to someone else?

**Cara:** Mad—and very disappointed.

**Mom:** Can you think of why she might have done that?

**Cara:** I don't know.

**Mom:** See if you can think of three reasons why Suzanne might have made you feel mad and very disappointed.

**Cara:** Maybe she was mad at me for something. Maybe she doesn't like me anymore. Maybe she got in trouble and was taking it out on me.

**Mom:** Good thinking. Can you think of something to do or say to let Suzanne know how you feel?

Asking Cara to think about why Suzanne would tell her secret to someone else was helpful to Cara. The next day, Cara asked Suzanne why she had acted the way she had. Suzanne explained that her teacher had yelled at her in front of the whole class for forgetting her homework and that she was very upset by this. Cara then understood that Suzanne had transferred her bad feelings toward her and didn't really mean to hurt her personally.

Cara told Suzanne she felt very hurt even so and that she couldn't be her friend if she couldn't trust her. Suzanne felt very bad that she had betrayed her friend's trust and promised not to do that again—and she didn't.

Sometimes the consequences of broken trust can go beyond hurt feelings. They can escalate into being teased by peers, doubling the impact of the betrayal.

Andrew, seven, tried to relieve some of his anxiety by confiding to his friend Ronald that he had scary dreams at night, and sometimes woke up crying. He thought he could trust Ronald, but Ronald ended up telling others about Andrew's dreams. As word got out, Andrew was tagged a "crybaby," a taunt that lasted for months. Now Andrew had two tasks: to let Ronald know how bad he felt about the betrayal and to get kids to stop teasing him.

After talking with his parents, Andrew recognized how hurt he was feeling. He decided the best way to solve his problem was to confront Ronald first. "Everyone's calling me names and it's because of you," Andrew said. "You started it, now you finish it." A startled and remorseful Ronald asked the kids to stop. Although it took time for the nickname to fade away, Andrew felt good that Ronald tried to rectify his mistake and knew that Ronald wouldn't intentionally hurt him again.

When children take action instead of passively sitting back and feeling bad inside, they turn problems into problems that can be solved. In the process, friendships may be saved that might otherwise have been lost. In fact, they may be strengthened.

---

When children take action instead of passively sitting back and feeling bad inside, they turn problems into problems that can be solved.

---

## "She Stabbed Me in the Back"— Stopping the Spread of Rumors

Theresa was one of the best students in the sixth grade: she was very bright, got all As, and worked very hard. After school, she went right home to study. She didn't have playdates. She didn't even join the other girls in the schoolyard during recess, preferring to sit by herself and read.

Over time, the other girls noticed how much Theresa kept to her-self, and they concluded that she was a snob. One girl in particular, Judy, seemed most annoyed. "Let's show her who's so smart," she told the others. Led by Judy, the girls waited until a day when Theresa was absent from school. Then they each wrote up a study sheet for a test they had a few days earlier and placed these crib sheets in Theresa's desk. When Theresa returned to school, the girls "found" the crib sheets and talked about how Theresa had cheated on the test until the teacher heard them. As they had hoped, Theresa got in big trouble. Though the girls felt gleeful, they kept their emotions under wraps and even managed to look sad that Theresa had been so "dishonest."

Theresa arrived home feeling devastated. Not only was she upset that she was in trouble for something she didn't do, but she felt sick at heart that her classmates could be so mean.

Her mom knew how important it was to help her daughter before her emotions escalated out of control. She wasn't sure how to help her daughter. She considered calling the teacher but realized that the teacher wouldn't believe Theresa's claim of innocence; after all, the teacher had confiscated the crib sheets. But Theresa's mom also realized that Theresa needed to learn to cope with this problem. Here's how she eventually talk-ed to her daughter:

> **Mom:** Your teacher tells me you cheated on your test. She found notes you made in your desk.
> **Theresa:** I didn't make any notes.
> **Mom:** How do think they got there?
> **Theresa:** *(starting to cry)* I don't know.
> **Mom:** I believe you. Can you think of a way to convince your teacher you didn't cheat?
> **Theresa:** *(still crying)* No. I can't. She wouldn't believe me anyway.
> **Mom:** I know you'll think of something. Take your time.

The next day, Theresa saw some girls looking at her and giggling as soon as she walked in the door. That's when she realized that these girls had planted the notes in her desk. When she arrived home, she told her mother what she'd discovered.

**Theresa:** Mom, some girls put the notes in my desk.

**Mom:** Why would they do that?

**Theresa:** They don't like me and they're mean.

**Mom:** Well, we have two problems here. One involves the teacher and one involves the kids. Do you know what the problems are?

**Theresa:** Yeah, I have to convince the teacher I didn't cheat and I have to make sure the kids never do that again.

**Mom:** OK. Let's start with the teacher. What can you do so she'll believe you didn't cheat?

**Theresa:** Tell her what the kids did.

**Mom:** What might happen if you do that?

**Theresa:** Oh yeah. They might get revenge.

**Mom:** What can you do so that won't happen?

**Theresa:** I could tell her to give me a new test and show her I don't have any notes.

**Mom:** That's good thinking. Now, let's talk about the other girls. Why do you think they want to hurt you so much?

**Theresa:** I don't know.

**Mom:** Think hard. Is there anything you did or said that might have set them off?

**Theresa:** I think they're jealous because I get better grades than they do.

**Mom:** How can you make them not feel so jealous?

**Theresa:** Maybe I can offer to help them with their homework.

**Mom:** You're a very good problem solver. How do you feel when you solve problems so well?

**Theresa:** Proud.

The next day, Theresa approached the teacher and told her what had happened—without mentioning any names—and offered to take the test again. When she did well, the teacher realized that Theresa had been telling the truth after all.

That took care of one problem. In terms of dealing with her classmates, Theresa realized that by keeping to herself at recess she appeared standoffish—even though that's not how she felt. She made an extra effort to join in during certain games. It wasn't always easy for her, but she tried.

She also began paying attention to which kids were having trouble with certain subjects. When she realized that one of the more popular girls in class was struggling to complete her math homework, Theresa offered to help her.

Now when her classmates talk about Theresa, it's about how helpful she is. And Theresa feels doubly smart—in school and with her peers.

## How to Help When Your Child Is Excluded

Kids of just about all ages tell me that being left out of the group is one of the things they fear most. Ten-year-old Randy came home from school crying because no boys invited him to join them at lunch. Eight-year-old Davida felt devastated because she wasn't invited to a friend's birthday party.

Having friends and feeling accepted by peers is critically important to both boys and girls. According to Gary Ladd, researcher at the University of Illinois, this need heightens as children grow, progressing through the primary grades.

When I encountered situations like these, my mother would say, "Don't worry about it. You won't even remember it ten years from now."

My mom genuinely wanted to comfort me and thought that she was, but even now I have a clear memory of not feeling comforted. I never told her this because I didn't want to hurt her feelings, but her words did nothing to assuage my pain.

Children need real help dealing with the many tangled issues that arise between friends. Offering empty assurance, glossing over the problem, or ignoring it will not help or make it go away. This is not a dilemma that can be solved quickly or easily.

Ten-year-old Ruth was frequently left off the invitation list and excluded from activities by the "popular kids." First her mom asked her how she was feeling about this. Ruth said that she felt sad about not being included in things, but she also felt comforted that her mother cared enough to talk to her about the subject. Next Mom asked, "What can you think of to do so you won't feel so bad about this?" Ruth thought for a long time, but she couldn't think of anything to say.

Later in the day, Ruth came to her mom and said, "Maybe I can try to find new friends. Maybe these kids aren't worth the trouble. I'm not going to go chasing them anymore." When Mom asked Ruth to think of someone else in the class she could be friends with, Ruth thought of Lori, whom she found out likes to garden. One day, Ruth asked Lori to plant seeds with her. Lori seemed interested, but she said she had a big project for homework and was having trouble with it. Ruth offered to help her, and Lori, surprised and appreciative, accepted the offer. Several days later, Lori invited Ruth to her garden, and they had fun planning out where to plant all the seeds. They talked a lot about school and what they each liked to do. Over time, as they became good friends, Lori introduced Ruth to her circle of friends. Ruth no longer felt excluded.

Ruth learned several important lessons from this experience: not to give up, not to feel bad about herself, and that she had the ability to turn a problem into a problem-solving opportunity. She also learned that it takes time to reach important goals, but it's often well worth the wait.

Most important, Ruth thought of this idea herself. Had her mother suggested this plan, would Ruth have been able to execute it with the same energy and conviction? Would she have experienced the same degree of success and pride?

# 12

# Talking with Kids About Safe Behaviors, Risky Behaviors, and Violence

## Helping Children Avoid Dangerous Situations

Dena, age seven, hated to wear her seat belt. Every time she got in the car, she'd squirm and cry. Though her parents explained to her why the seat belt was necessary, she didn't hear them. Her parents had to struggle to buckle her in, and after they did, no one felt good—her parents were exhausted, and Dena felt as if she'd been overpowered.

Kent, age four, kept trying to break away from his mom when they approached a busy street. His mom told me that when he darts out like that, she pulls him back and yells, "Don't ever do that again! Don't you know a car could run over you?" Sometimes, she continued, she even spanks him right on the spot. Then she elaborated, "The only time I spank him is when he does really dangerous things, like trying to break away from me at a busy street."

Kent's mom is giving in to her sense of frustration. Children are unable to think about what they're doing when they're being yelled at or spanked. Even explaining the reasons won't help. Children need to feel as if *they* have discovered why they should avoid potentially dangerous situations. Using the example of running into the street, here's how you can help.

Ask your child, "What might happen if you run into a busy street?" If he says he doesn't know, you can guide him without telling him. You can ask, "What might happen if you are in the street and a car comes and you can't get out of the way?"

Your child will now probably respond that he could get hit by a car. One child added, "I could get hurt and have to go to the hospital."

Now ask, "How might Daddy and I feel if you got hurt and had to go to the hospital?"

Then ask, "How would *you* feel if that happened?"

Finally, ask, "What can you do so you won't get hit by a car?"

Kent thought about this last question and then said, "I can stay with you, and not go out into the road."

His mother replied, "I'm proud of you." Next time Kent began to break away from his mom as they crossed the street, he suddenly stopped, looked up at her, and whispered, "not in the street."

Because Dena is older, her parents had a more sophisticated conversation with her about seat belts. First, they acknowledged that Dena felt uncomfortable wearing the seat belt. She found it annoying. Sometimes they did, too, they told her. But then they asked her, "Why do you think cars have seat belts? What might happen if you didn't fasten yourself in?"

Dena acknowledged that she could get thrown around inside the car and bump her head on the seat in front of her or on the window; and it would hurt and she'd feel sad—she might even have to go to the hospital.

Her father then said, "How might you feel if that happens?"

Dena admitted that she'd be unhappy. "So is it a good idea or not a good idea to wear your seat belt?" he asked.

"A good idea," Dena said.

There are lots of potentially dangerous situations kids can get into: touching a hot stove, standing in front of a moving swing, riding a bike too fast. After being helped to think about possible consequences and how they and others would feel, you can shorten the dialogue with just one question: "Can you think of a *different* place to put your hand?" "Can you think of a *different* place to stand?" "Can you think of a *different* way to ride your bike?" Children will respond to questions like these, and most of the time, no more will need to be said.

We can't control what our children do every minute. But we can help them think, early in their lives, about what is and is not safe, so we can trust them to take responsibility for their actions and to make safe decisions now and as they mature.

## Keeping Your Kids Away from the Wrong Crowd

"Mom, this is Ellen," says eleven-year-old Nancy, who is clearly delighted that her new friend came home with her after school. As the girls have a snack in the kitchen, Rae, Nancy's mom, hears them whispering and giggling. When she leaves the room, she overhears their conversation—and Ellen using language Rae finds inappropriate. And come to think of it, Ellen's shirt and pants are awfully tight and show a lot of midriff. And is she really wearing four earrings in her left ear?

When kids are young, it's easy to know all their friends, and even the parents. But when kids begin elementary school, and especially middle school, they spend many hours away from your watchful gaze. Their world begins to widen, which is a good thing, but in the process you naturally lose some of the control you had over who came into their world. It's natural to begin to worry about the friends your child makes. You know how important friends are and how susceptible kids are to peer pressure.

You also know that if you were to suggest to your daughter that she stop being friends with Ellen, it will only make Ellen seem more attractive. What can you do?

If your child is caught up in what you think may be a destructive relationship, find some time alone with her and ask her some questions:

"How do you feel when you're around those kids?"
"What is it about them that you like?"
"Do you like the way you feel around them?"
"What can happen if you stay friends with those kids?"
"Do you want that to happen?"
"What can you do so that it won't happen?"
"How will you feel then?"

You'd be surprised to realize that many children don't think about the issues raised above. Rae was. She discussed these problem--solving questions with Nancy not once but several more times. At first, she was dismayed—Nancy didn't give the answers she'd hoped for. Instead, her daughter insisted that she really liked Ellen and that "nothing" would happen. "Don't worry so much, Mom," Nancy said firmly.

It was hard for Rae not to worry. But she trusted that she'd given Nancy plenty to think about and bided her time. A few weeks later, she began to see some changes in her daughter. Nancy talked about how Ellen was pressuring her to do things she really didn't want to do—like not handing in homework, "hanging out" after school, and even wearing those "pierced things." Nancy thought more now about what was right for her—and that maybe this was a friendship she didn't really want after all.

At best, asking the above questions can help your child achieve an inner strength she didn't know she had. When twelve-year-old Leila started sulking around the house, for example, her mom asked her what was wrong. "My friends are bothering me, and I don't know how to get them to stop," Leila said. "They keep asking me to do stuff, bad stuff. They want me to go with them to bad neighborhoods, and at first I thought they were just kidding. They're my friends, but they're trying to destroy me, or get me in trouble."

"Just tell them you're not allowed to go," her mother suggested. But that didn't address how disheartened and disillusioned Leila felt. What added salt to her wound was the fact that her "friends" had threatened her, telling her that if she didn't go with them, they'd never talk to her again and tell other kids not to, either.

"How do you feel when you're around those kids?" her mom asked.

"Scared. Sick inside."

"What is it about them that you like?" her mother asked next.

Leila had a hard time answering, but finally said, "They're cool. They're popular."

But when Mom asked, "Do you like the way you feel around them?" Leila realized she did not. To the question, "What can happen if you stay friends with those kids?" Leila knew she could get hurt, or in trouble. And she knew that she didn't want that to happen.

Now Mom asked, "What can you do so that won't happen?"

"Find new friends to protect me, and run away when I see those mean girls."

"And how will you feel then?" asked Mom.

"Relieved. Still a little scared. But a little better."

Most kids, like Leila, really do want to talk with their parents about issues like these even if, like Nancy, they seem resistant to the conversation at first. You can let your child know how you feel about friends who could hurt her. If you help her think about what might happen, you won't have to tell her why. Equally important, they'll be better prepared to resist peer pressure and other unforeseen consequences as they approach those tumultuous teenage years.

## Talking About Drugs

"Just say no!"

A few years ago, we were told this was all our kids had to say to keep from getting involved with drugs.

How well did the slogan work? The 2001 National Household Survey on Drug Abuse reported that 15.9 million Americans were illicit drug users—with many starting as early as age twelve.

Clearly, it takes more than a slogan to help younger kids understand why experimenting with drugs isn't in their best interest. Slogans aren't effective for several reasons. For one thing, kids tend to tune them out. Slogans don't address the problem of kids who can't just say no, perhaps because they are afraid of what might happen if they do. And they don't help kids think of options to reach whatever goal it is that's luring them to the drugs in the first place. Finally, slogans seduce parents into thinking that the drug problem has an easy solution.

There is no easy answer. Kids try drugs for a host of complicated reasons. Some of it has to do with peer pressure, and the fact that they don't know how to cope with that pressure. Or they may be lured by a sensation-seeking motive, not thinking about the consequences of their actions.

Perhaps the most important reason to discount slogans is because they shortchange kids; that is, they don't encourage kids to think for themselves.

Yet children who have critical-thinking skills are the best equipped to stay away from drugs.

You can work to prevent your child from using drugs by developing these critical-thinking skills, and you can start much earlier than you probably realize. In fact, the hard work of prevention has to begin years before drugs actually enter your child's life. My own research, conducted over the past thirty years, shows that by age four, children can be, or can learn to become, good problem solvers.

For instance, I observed two children arguing over an action figure. The argument escalated until one boy said to the other, "You can't come to my birthday party."

"So what?" said the other boy. "I don't care."

Does he really not care about being rejected by one of his peers? And if he can shrug off being hurt in this way now, will he continue to feel this way? What happens when he's older and he learns that drugs can seriously harm him? Will he still have his "I don't care" attitude? And if he hasn't learned to care about his own feelings, how will he learn to care about the feelings of others?

I have found that a few very simple questions can help children as young as four and five consider what they are doing and the impact of their behavior:

"What's the problem?" (This helps children identify in words the problem that needs solving.)

"What happened when you two started fighting over the toy?" (This helps children think about the consequences of their actions.)

"How do you think he feels when you fight like that?" (This often elicits answers like, "He feels mad.")

"How did *you* feel when he told you not to come to his party?" (This often elicits answers like, "I was sad.")

"Can you think of a different way to solve the problem?" (This helps children think of alternate solutions to the problem, such as, "I can let him play with my toy," "I can tell him I'll play with it for just a little while more," and "I can tell him I'll be his friend.")

You may be asking yourself what birthday parties and rejections have to do with not taking drugs. Though it may not be obvious, there is a clear link. We know that the children who are most likely to abuse drugs when they get older are those who are unable to solve the typical, everyday problems in their lives. That's because they don't know how to make decisions—they don't know how to articulate the problem, explore it, think of solutions, and anticipate obstacles or other outcomes. If we start teaching those as young as preschool age how to solve the problems important to them—like how to be invited to a birthday party, and how to get to play with a wanted toy—they'll develop a way of thinking about their problems that will be portable. That is, as they grow, they will adapt their problem-solving abilities and apply them to age-appropriate difficulties, such as how to resist peers who pressure them to try drugs.

Though Nelson was only eight, he already knew about the dangers of drugs even though they hadn't yet entered his life. When I asked him what could happen, he had a host of answers: "You could go swimming and drown. You could get sick and miss too much school. You could hurt your friend 'cause you'd be so out of it." When asked how he could resist a peer who tried to pressure him, he answered, "Tell him I don't want to die. Then get his friends to pressure him." When asked what he meant by that, he said, "It's better if five of us tell him than only me. Then he'd really leave me alone."

Children who learn critical-thinking skills early in life will grow up to be thinking, feeling human beings. They will be more successful at making real friends who will not pressure them into making unhealthy choices, will be able to make responsible decisions in light of their potential consequences, and will feel pride in their successes instead of frustration over their failures. They will have less need to succumb to the pressures of doing what they don't want to do from "friends" they don't want to have. They will have an internal sense of feeling good so they won't need an artificial high. They will care what happens to them, and will come to care about others, too.

In other words, children who know how to solve problems important to them when they're younger will be able to solve more complex problems important to them when they're older. What a huge difference there is between teaching kids to think about these issues and telling them to "Just say no."

## Talking About Smoking and Alcohol

What may trouble you when you listen to the news or read the paper isn't simply that more and more young people are smoking, but that the age at which kids first try cigarettes is plummeting. Now kids in middle school identify themselves as smokers. According to a recent National Youth Tobacco Survey, 12.8 percent of middle schoolers and 34.8 percent of high school students use some form of tobacco.

The last thing you want to do is threaten to ground your child, question him relentlessly about whether or not he's smoking, or lecture him about the dangers. You know in your heart that these strategies will only backfire.

Rather than talk *at* your child, find out what he already knows. And by asking questions, you may well snuff out his desire for a cigarette before he first lights up.

Here's how Sibby, eleven, answered questions I posed to her:

*Why do you want to smoke cigarettes?*
"I guess I want to be cool. And popular. Most girls who smoke are the popular ones. And the people you see smoking in movies are cool, too."

*Why is smoking not a good idea?*
"Smoking blackens your lungs and you'd have to have an operation, and then you'd have only one lung. Also, your breath stinks when you smoke, and people don't like to be around you. It causes depression 'cause you're never happy without a cigarette."

*What hopes and dreams do you have for the future?*
"I want to do something with animals. Maybe be a marine biologist."

*How can smoking interfere with these dreams?*
"I wouldn't have energy to go scuba diving. And all of the buildings would

be smoke-free in a few years and I couldn't go into any of them. People wouldn't want to work with me 'cause I'd smell like an ashtray."

*What are some ways you can begin to reach your goals now?*
"Get good grades and test scores. That way I can get into the college I want to and study marine biology."

*How can you try to be as cool and popular as the girls who smoke but in your own way?*
"I can be friendly and generous to people, and try to make new friends. I can be interested in what they're interested in. That's what makes kids really popular."

Questions such as these can plant an early seed. While Sibby may have thought about someday smoking, her new insights make me think she never will. Perhaps questions like these will help to prevent your child from smoking, too.

You can use the same approach—asking your child what he knows before launching into a lecture—when talking about alcohol. For instance, twelve-year-old Lawrence's best friend, Sean, has two older brothers, aged sixteen and eighteen, who are already into heavy drinking, and Sean's parents don't seem too concerned about this. When Lawrence told his mom that one of the older brothers tried to talk him into having a drink, his mom exploded, characterizing the family as "lowlifes" and forbidding Lawrence to go over there anymore. "I don't want you ever to associate with that boy again," she shouted, "do you understand?!"

Dad sympathized with his wife but didn't want to lose control. He also wanted to hear what Lawrence had to say. Though his more laid-back approach angered his wife, he insisted on waiting for an opportune moment to talk with Lawrence. That moment arose when father and son were watching a ballgame together on TV, and a beer commercial came on. "What do you think about kids who drink?" he asked Lawrence.

Lawrence wasn't feeling afraid or defensive, so he confided in his father that Sean's brother offered him a beer. "But I said no," Lawrence explained. "When he saw I really wouldn't try it, he finally left me alone."

"Why did you say no?" his dad asked.

"'Cause I don't want to get sick," Lawrence said. "And anyway, I probably wouldn't like how it tastes."

Dad just nodded. From this brief conversation, he realized that he didn't have to tell his son about the problems associated with alcohol; Lawrence already knew.

And Lawrence's mom realized that she didn't have to forbid Lawrence from seeing his friend. "There's no point in discouraging Lawrence from playing with Sean," she explained to me. "Sean's not doing him any harm. I know he'll be exposed to this kind of thing later on anyway. Anyway, this is a good training ground for him to think about these kinds of things. And I know Lawrence will talk to us because he knows we trust him and trust how he thinks."

I asked Lawrence's dad why he didn't call Sean's parents and inform them of their son's drinking. "They seem so lax about it, I figured they wouldn't do anything anyway," Lawrence's dad said. In addition, he feared that such a phone call might anger Sean's parents, which would then have an impact on the boys' friendship. If you find yourself in a similar situation, you can judge whether a call to the child's parents would help.

Preteens who are helped to think about important issues such as smoking cigarettes and drinking alcohol—and who are *not* bombarded with dos and don'ts—are much more likely to decide for themselves not to start smoking or drinking, or to stop before it's too late.

## Talking with Preteens About Sex

Are you the parent of a preteen who's worried about whether she'll become sexually active at too young an age? Do you want to discuss the issue with her but feel unsure of what to say? According to the statistics, the sooner you talk to your daughter, the better. The National Campaign to Prevent Teen Pregnancy reports that one in five U.S. teens under the age of fifteen has had sexual intercourse, one in seven sexually experienced fourteen-year-old girls become pregnant, while only about one-third of their parents knew their daughter had had sex.

This is a problem parents of boys have to confront as well. Engaging in sex at a young age isn't just a girl's problem anymore. Teenage boys run the risk of contracting herpes, HIV-AIDS, and other sexually transmitted diseases as well.

Most likely, your preteen won't think about disease or any of the other risks of premature sex. When teenagers engage in sex, it's often for a number of complex and often interrelated reasons: to feel grown-up, popular, or needed; to keep pace with their peers; to release pent-up anger or stress; and to get back at a world that seems stacked against them. No matter how many statistics you cite or how airtight your arguments, you and your child are talking at cross-purposes.

It is possible to prevent these kinds of problems from happening to your teenage child by talking to him or her about it *now*. What will help keep your preteen from engaging in this potentially dangerous activity? From my perspective, the answer is his ability to plan ahead and to consider what might happen next, how he and others might feel about the consequences, and what else he might do to satisfy his needs.

Here are some ways you can talk to your children so that they can take control of their lives instead of letting life take control of them:

- Ask them what they already know about sexual activity, both safe and unsafe.
- Fill in the gaps in their knowledge. They may believe, for instance, that condoms offer more protection than they in fact do, or that oral sex is risk free.
- Ask them to think about the consequences of unsafe sex, and how these consequences could interfere with their future plans and dreams.
- Help them think of other ways to satisfy their emotional and physical needs.
- Ask them to think of a way to say "no" if pressured to engage in sex.

Eleven-year-old Anna came home from a party at which her girl-friends were talking about boys and what it's like to go out with a boy.

Anna admitted that she was a little worried about feeling pressured by a boy. Here's how her mother pursued the conversation:

**Mom:** Why do you think some girls your age might say yes to a boy who wants to have sex?

**Anna:** To feel cool and popular.

**Mom:** And what are some good reasons not to do that?

**Anna:** They could get pregnant or get AIDS. And they wouldn't like themselves because they're doing something they really don't want to.

**Mom:** Good thinking. Anna, what are your hopes and dreams for the future?

**Anna:** I want to be a forensic scientist, like the ones on TV.

**Mom:** If you should get pregnant too soon, how would that affect your hopes and dreams?

**Anna:** I'd be stuck with a baby and I couldn't take care of it. I couldn't follow my hopes and dreams. Especially if I got AIDS.

**Mom:** You said that girls might say yes to a boy to feel cool and popular. Can you think of other ways to be cool and popular now?

**Anna:** I could try to get really good at something, like soccer. And be a good sport about it.

**Mom:** Can you think of a way to say no to someone who might pressure you?

**Anna:** I can tell him I have other, more important things to do.

Anna showed me that it is indeed possible to talk with kids well before their teenage years about significant life decisions. And with youngsters actually engaging in such risky behaviors as sexual activity at younger and younger ages, it is more important than ever to help your child think about these issues now.

When girls think about how an impetuous decision could derail their future plans, they often find it easier to resist any temptation and, like Anna, figure out a way to say no to boys who pressure them. In turn, boys can learn to develop empathy for any would-be partner who could suffer irreparable consequences.

## Are Video Games and Violent TV Shows Too Real?

Does your son spend hours playing video games? Does he favor those in which he gets to shoot at, blow up, or otherwise destroy human figures? Are you worried that playing these games may incline your child to resort to violence in real life?

Many parents share these fears. They're also afraid that too much exposure to violent video games and violent TV shows may cause their children to have violent fantasies. Some parents, in an effort to exert greater control, have banned them from their home entirely.

While experts have been trying to gauge the impact of violent media on real-life behavior, the results have proven inconclusive. One new study by L. Rowell Heusmann and his colleagues has shown that six- to ten-year-olds who watch violence on TV are at risk for aggression when studied fifteen years later, but primarily when the child identifies with the aggressive TV characters and perceives the observed aggression as real. But while you're waiting for more experts to weigh in, you can begin to help your child tackle the issue of video games and violence in other media.

Though you may be tempted to simply prohibit him from playing these games, it isn't the most effective strategy. In fact, it often backfires. First, it only serves to turn the games into "forbidden fruit," which is even more attractive. In addition, while you may monitor what types of games your child plays at home, you have much less control when he visits friends or takes trips to the arcade at the nearest mall.

To raise a child who's thoughtful about the games he plays and why he enjoys them, ask him what he thinks of video games.

I've had this conversation with many children. One ten-year-old boy told me, "Video games are just fiction. They're fun. It's cool to play them. And they help me with my hand-eye coordination. That makes me feel good."

When I asked him if he thought that playing video games might encourage him to hurt anyone in real life, he said, "I would never hurt anyone in real life. I could get in trouble, and I would lose my friends. You can't lose friends in a video game."

Another boy, also ten, agreed. "Video games aren't real. They're just fun." When I asked him if he thought that playing video games could make kids turn violent, he confidently assured me that they couldn't. "Once you beat the game," he explained, "that's the end. There's no more to do. It's no big deal." He did tell me why he thought that a classmate—a bully who had no friends—liked these games: "They probably make him feel better. When he plays, he's in control. In real life, he's not."

This boy touched on an issue many parents are concerned about: control. Parents worry that the games allow their children to wield too much power over who gets hurt, in what way, and for how long. "It's no big deal," kids say. But many parents don't agree.

To encourage your child to develop a healthy perspective on the games, talk about them with your child. Watch the TV shows that include violence with her, too. In addition to the questions I asked above, here are some others you can pose:

"How do you feel when someone gets hurt in real life?"
"How do you think the other person feels when he's hurt?"
"If you feel angry in real life, what can you do so that you won't hurt anyone?"

Questions such as these are especially helpful for youngsters who are unable to distinguish video games or TV shows from reality or who may appear to actually enjoy the violence. That's an important distinction—and one that he won't learn to draw if you simply ban him from playing the games.

Another option is to watch one or two of these shows with your child and use them as a teaching tool. Ask such questions as:

"What happened when he punched the other guy?"
"How did the guy feel?"
"How do you think the man who punched him really felt inside?"
"What else could happen when people punch each other like that?"
"Can you think of a *different* way they could solve this problem?"

Banning violent video games or violent TV shows may or may not allay your concern about potential violence, now or later. In truth, we seem to be in the midst of a violence epidemic. In the year 2000, the Center for Disease Control reported that more than four hundred thousand youths between the ages of ten and nineteen were injured in violent episodes, many requiring hospitalization. Equally disturbing is a report by the Office of Juvenile Justice and Delinquency that the murder rate for girls, while still low compared to boys, is up 64 percent from what it was ten years ago.

Think about how you want to talk to your children about violence in games and on TV. Consider both sides of the coin. Given that a complete ban might make them more alluring, you might decide to use these kinds of media as vehicles to help your child develop empathy for the very behaviors you want to prevent.

## Teaching Kids Not to Hate

Noah, although only seven, was aware, in his own way, that we were at war with Iraq. During that time, I asked him his feelings about our being there, and he answered, "I don't feel cozy. The kids over there might get hurt. The bad guys would blame it on us but they should blame it on themselves 'cause they told the kids to go to war."

Noah likened the war to what he learns about bullying in school. "Only kids who fight get hurt. We won't get hurt 'cause we don't fight." Then Noah came up with a plan: "We should build a secret building with schools and malls and bathrooms and knock down all the buildings [in Iraq] except the secret building. Then, when all the bad guys get killed, they'll have a secret building to start a new city and the kids will be safe."

Gina, twelve, was concerned that innocent people in Iraq might get hurt. Nine-year-old Dan was concerned that people in Iraq needed to feel free and safe. He discussed the issue with his dad, Oliver, who had carefully considered both the pros and cons of going to war.

Some parents think it best not to discuss the war or other traumatic events with their kids because it could scare them. As one mom told me, "They shouldn't have to deal with this." Noah, Gina, and Dan have convinced me otherwise. When parents talk to their kids at the appropriate level of understanding, answering their questions briefly but honestly, not only do their kids feel less anxious, but they are free to think about people getting hurt. These children are not consumed with hate for the enemy. They express concern about the welfare of people they do not know.

Have the September 11 terrorist attacks and the wars in Afghanistan and Iraq caused our children to think and feel differently about people of the Muslim faith? If any of their classmates happen to be Arabs or of Arab descent, what are they thinking about them? How can we teach our kids not to hate?

It's of critical importance that children don't learn to hate, distrust, or fear any neighbors or classmates who look "foreign." Now is a good opportunity to help teach our kids that not everyone who resembles the terrorists or the "bad guys" from the Middle East is bad.

To help children sort out their feelings about Muslims or other ethnic groups from the Middle East, start by talking in general terms about how people are the same and how they are different. Start with your own family. Ask your child, "How are you and I the *same*? How are we *different*?"

As young as three, children can recognize that we all have two eyes and two arms, among other shared features. Yet they can also make key distinctions. As one three-year-old put it, "Mommy is big and I am little." By age four, children can understand, "Mommy is not a man. I am not a man. That's how we are the same."

Kids love to think about how other members of the family are the same and different. You can then expand the game to include their friends and classmates. If your child knows anyone from a Middle Eastern ethnic group, include that person in the game, and your child may come to see that person in a new light.

In their delightful book *The Berenstain Bears' New Neighbors*, Stan and Jan Berenstain help very young children learn that it's important to find out more about people before assuming they're not going to be friendly or nice. They illustrate how the new "panda bear" family who moves in next door begins putting up what Papa Bear thought looked like a "spite fence"—a row of sticks that "bad neighbors put up just for spite," explaining that this kind of fence keeps people from seeing what they're doing.

As it turned out, the "spite fence" was really a row of bamboo, their neighbors' favorite food. And their mom, Mrs. Panda, is a great bamboo cook who has about fifty recipes. The two families become good friends and share their favorite foods, each learning to like the other's cuisine. This excellent story encourages children to reflect on what they can learn from people only after they get to know them better.

Thinking about how people are the same and different, and what they might learn about new people, are good exercises for young children. If you have older children, talk to them more directly about their feelings about people from the Middle East—people your child may have become suspicious of in light of current world events.

One way to prompt them to reevaluate their feelings is to encourage them to learn more about people from these cultures. A book like *Celebrating Ramadan*, by Diane Hoyt-Goldsmith, can help. This engaging book, filled with wonderful photographs, follows a Muslim family through the celebration of Ramadan, explaining the tradition that brings families together to reaffirm their faith. Your child will be able to see how Muslim families live their lives in ways that are similar to ours. They will also be able to talk about the things that divide us without feeling threatened by those differences.

If your child is ostracized for being "different," try using the problem-solving approach. Charise, a fifth-grader, was rejected by her African American classmates because, as she told her mom, "My skin is too light." She frequently came home crying, "I have no friends. No one will play with me. They say I'm ugly." Both her teacher and her mom tried to help, giving her suggestions and advice on what to say and how to say it. Nothing worked—until she and her mom began problem solving. Then Charise came up with a plan. She invited some girls to a birthday party at her house. Only a few of her classmates came, but with those who did, she played the "same and different" game that she learned from her mom. "I'm the same as you because I'm in the fifth grade, I have to learn math and stuff, and I live in the same neighborhood as you." Then she added, "I'm different from you because I have light skin. I really feel sad and hurt when you don't play with me." One of the kids was so moved by this that she told everyone else to be Charise's friend. Charise is now sought out and has lots of friends. All because she was able to think of what to do—and how to do it—for herself.

Do children who live in homes where their feelings are cared about and whose thoughts are respected grow up better prepared for the challenges of an unpredictable world? Do children who are raised to have empathy grow up not wanting to hurt themselves or others? Would the boys who killed classmates and teachers at Columbine High School in Littleton, Colorado, have acted as they did if they'd been taught not to hate? If only they could have thought of another way; if only they could have rejected violence as the means to solving their problems; if only the adults at their school had been sensitive to how these boys were ostracized and ridiculed. Would promoting empathy and teaching problem-solving skills to everyone in the school have prevented this from happening at all?

Imagine the kind of world we would have if we had more Noahs, Ginas, and Dans, who are learning early in life not to hate, and more Charises, who have learned how to defuse hatred. Wouldn't this country be a more compassionate and humane place to live?

A few years back, after Rodney King was mercilessly beaten by policemen for what they thought was a crime in the making, he asked a very poignant question, "Can't we all get along?" In a society where racism is still a chronic and pervasive problem, and now a world of violence and terror, we must teach our kids not to hate.

# PART 3

■

# Nurturing
# Relationships

*Parents who think more about what their children do also think more
about what they themselves do.*

The first place a child learns how to get along with others is in the
home. But in this fast-paced age, more moms are working, one kid has
soccer practice and doesn't get home until seven o'clock, way beyond
the time the four-year-old can wait for dinner, and sometimes Dad gets
home in time for dinner and sometimes he does not. In the midst of all
this turmoil, someone comes up with a problem that to Mom and Dad
seems so trivial and they want to ignore—but is so momentous to the
kids.

In Part 2, I talked about how some typical behavior problems can be
nipped in the bud to prevent more serious and long-lasting problems
later on. Part 3 focuses on how families can tighten their bond, create
trust, and work together to help children develop the strength and confidence to meet the challenges they will face throughout their lives. I will
also show you how your family can provide a safe haven for helping your
kids cope with conflicts at home, skills they can take with them and use
elsewhere—at school, for example.

Some of the conflicts at home are between parents themselves—when they disagree, for example, on how to raise the kids. Others may be created by the parents, such as when they don't keep a promise they made. Still others, for youngsters who have brothers or sisters, revolve around issues of sibling rivalry.

Sibling rivalry has many facets. Psychologists Lynn Katz and her colleagues have studied how sibling relationships offer children unique opportunities for learning about conflict. One sibling, usually the older one, has more power, and conflicts occur frequently between sibs. Children in grades four and five report an average of 4.7 fights per day with sibs, averaging eight minutes, with bad feelings lasting about six minutes after the fight was over.

Importantly, sibling rivalry can be quite constructive. Children can learn to negotiate, compromise, take turns, and learn to consider and coordinate each other's point of view. They can learn that people have different opinions and feelings about things.

Unlike peers, choice of siblings is not voluntary, nor is the opportunity to discontinue the relationship—at least for now. The stability of this relationship may free children to explore their own wants and needs and how they fit with wants and needs of others.

Deborah Vandell and Mark Bailey from the University of Wisconsin caution, however, that not all sibling conflicts are so constructive. Conflicts may continue beyond the issues that first caused them and are not likely to be resolved by means of negotiation in ways that both parties can accept. While constructive conflicts enhance understanding of each other's point of view and problem-solving skills, destructive conflicts do not—and these can lead to hostile, alienated relationships later on in life. Unresolved sibling conflicts contribute to more behavior problems, poorer peer relationships, and greater difficulties in school.

Are no conflicts at all healthy? Vandell and Bailey report that only about 10 percent of children studied had no conflicts at all with their sibs. The siblings in this group, while fiercely protective of each other and tuned in to each other's thoughts and feelings, were less concerned about the wants and needs of others, either peers or adults, and ended up not having friends. And what about constructive conflicts? Georgia

Witkin, in her book *KidStress,* reports that siblings who engage in constructive conflicts appreciate "having someone around who knows how I feel sometimes," someone who will "watch out for you and stick up for you," and be "a good friend forever."

How might parents influence how constructive or destructive sibling conflicts might be? Parents who argue frequently can affect the general emotional climate in the household, and this kind of added stress can influence relationships between siblings. Parents who use primarily punitive techniques of discipline are in more frequent  conflict with their child, which adds to the frequency and intensity of conflicts among sibs. And parents who intervene too quickly may deprive their children of the opportunity to learn how to solve problems with others, now and later.

I begin Part 3 by showing you how parents can resolve family issues by finding time for each other in this fast-paced age, keeping promises in order to develop trust, and settling spousal disagreements about how to raise the kids to minimize your child's playing one parent against the other. I then show you how to enhance the probability that normal, healthy issues of sibling rivalry will not escalate into destructive conflicts.

I conclude Part 3 by demonstrating how skills learned within the safe haven of the home can be used when inevitable conflicts arise outside it—with peers. This ability is crucial because my own research suggests that good problem-solving skills help children make good friends, and researchers Jeffrey Parker and Steven Asher report that having good friends is a powerful predictor of later success in life.

# 13

# Family Ties

## Making Family Quality Time

If your family is like that of most Americans, you probably need a wall-sized calendar on which to keep track of everyone's day-to-day activities. Mondays the kids have hockey practice and rehearse for the school play; Tuesdays Mom stays late at the office; Wednesdays Dad meets with his sales group. Which means that dinner becomes a "grab what you can, when you can" affair. And as for weekends, they become so clogged with trying to fit in all the errands that a week can pass without any family time at all. In fact, it sometimes seems as if the only time you're all home together is when you're asleep.

You know you need to make some time to talk, to just be together, to eat a meal together, even to watch a favorite television show together. But how?

Here are a few suggestions.

First, adjust your expectations. You may not be able to arrange for family dinners five times a week or even three, so just try for once or twice a week, at least at first. But make the most of that time. Keep the television off and just encourage each person to talk about what is on his or her mind at the moment.

This may seem obvious, but a friend of mine told me that when she was a kid, her father insisted on watching the news during dinner because "that was the only time he could catch up on what's going on in the world." Even today, when people have the option of taping programs that are broadcast during dinner to watch later in the evening, many still choose to watch and eat. And if parents aren't watching the news, the TV is on for the kids. When I stayed with two preteens for a week while their parents were out of town, I couldn't talk to them during dinner because they had to watch "their shows."

How can you make the most of the time you have together? Some families go for a stroll after dinner. Make it a ritual—every time you eat dinner together, follow up with a walk. Or set aside Saturday or Sunday mornings to fly a kite. Plan a picnic. Go to the museum. Or just take a walk to the store for ice cream.

Family time doesn't always have to be scheduled or involve elaborate activities. Talk with your child while he's doing his chores. Ask him how he's feeling while he's doing the dishes, cleaning his room, or helping to fold the laundry. In this way, chores serve a double purpose: while you're encouraging communication, he'll feel as if the chores are less burdensome.

Take advantage of your time in the car, bus, or train en route to various activities. Kids often open up while traveling—it may have to do with leaving the hassles of family life behind, giving them time to stretch out and relax, or the lulling motion of the car. In any case, many parents find this a great time for heart-to-heart talks.

Another way to make good use of limited time is to not be too preoccupied with your own thoughts when you are with your child. Even though Claudia picked up her daughter LeeAnn from her piano lesson right after work, when she still had plenty on her mind, Claudia still listened to all LeeAnn told her about what she'd learned that day, what song she had to practice for next week, and what her piano teacher was wearing. Claudia talked to her daughter about how she felt when she took piano lessons as a girl. And when they got home, LeeAnn couldn't wait to go to the piano and show Mom what she learned. It was as if their talk were a continuation of the lesson, all because Claudia could put aside her cares about work.

In the same vein, your child may want to talk to you about things that are upsetting her. Perhaps she didn't get chosen for the soccer team or she had a quarrel with her friend. If your time is really limited, make it a point to talk to her about these things—you can suggest a time you're together anyway, such as while she's setting the table for dinner. By sharing frustrations and disappointments you experienced as a kid, you may help her through tough times, too. When you make time to talk to your child about things that are important to your child at this moment, he'll want to talk to you about things that are important to him in the future.

Carve out a little time every day and your family will discover a lode of camaraderie and trust. No matter how brief, time with one another is valuable and important. It matters less *what* you do together than the fact that you *are* together.

## Work Family Time into Your Work Schedule

Some parents work during the day and get home early enough to spend time with their kids in the evening. Others work hours that make it harder for them to see their kids as much as they'd like.

Fred, for instance, is a desk clerk working the three-to-eleven shift in a high-rise apartment building. It's so difficult for him to spend time with his two preteen daughters that they've taken to calling him "Uncle Dad." He's at work when they come home from school. He can't join them for dinner or get involved with their activities or homework. The girls don't see Fred on weekends either, because they're off doing preteen things like going to the movies and the mall.

Although Fred doesn't want to interfere with his daughters' weekend activities, he feels left out of their lives. His wife, Betty, feels like a single parent, and the girls feel like they don't have a dad. Yet Fred has to work the shift he draws. What can a family in this situation do?

First, take advantage of Saturday and Sunday mornings before anyone leaves the house. Make breakfast for your kids. Talk to them about what they did during the week and their plans for the coming week. Tell them about your job and the people you meet. Kids love hearing about their parents' jobs and lives away from home. It's fascinating for them to imagine you leading a different life than the one you do as their mother or father. Talk about an incident that arose with a coworker, or an argument you settled, or a problem you helped solve.

That turns out to be just what Fred did. He told me a story he passed on to his kids about a woman who tried to sneak a very tiny dog into the building by placing it inside her purse—a tactic she felt was necessary because the building did not allow animals. He told his kids how bad he felt but that he had to escort the woman out of the building. When I asked him how he knew she had a dog, he smiled and said, "Because the purse barked." The woman, he explained to his kids, was irate and argued that the dog was little and wouldn't hurt anyone. Fred took this opportunity to ask his kids why they thought their father had to do what he did.

His nine-year-old answered, "'Cause if it was a rule, no dogs, you'd get fired." And his eleven-year-old added, "He might bite somebody and you'd be responsible for it." That thought gave the nine-year-old a new idea, "What if somebody was allergic to dogs and sneezed in the elevator; everyone in the elevator would get sick."

Fred also shared stories about how he helps people. One man just moved into town and didn't know anybody. When Fred found out that the newcomer was a musician, he told him about a banjo player on the fifth floor and said that he'd try to introduce them. The new person appreciated this potential connection, and Fred felt good about that. The conversation sparked his eleven-year-old to talk about how she showed a new girl around school and how they became best friends.

If you open up to your kids about moments you experience on the job, your kids will open up to you about their experiences at school, at home, or anywhere they may be.

You can communicate with your kids even when you don't see each other. Ask them to leave you notes, and do the same in return. Buy a supply of sticky notes and leave them on the fridge or some other agreed-upon place, like your pillow or perhaps on the bathroom mirror. Reply to their notes in the same way.

Harry, for example, is a police officer who often works the late shift. His daughter Renee, eleven, was petitioning for a new leather coat, which Harry denied. He felt that she was too young to take good care of it and worried that she'd leave it at the movies, as she'd done in the past with other coats. But he always felt too rushed to really talk with her about this because of his schedule.

That's when Renee got creative. She stuck a picture of the leather coat she'd cut out of the newspaper under the lid of the toilet seat.

When Harry lifted up the lid, he did a double take. At first he was annoyed that his daughter was such a pest—couldn't she leave him alone even in the bathroom?—but gradually his anger faded into pride as he acknowledged her ingenuity and resourcefulness. "How can I respond to this?" he thought to himself. As he left the bathroom, four options occurred to him. He could ignore it completely, giving Renee a sense of hopelessness so she would give up and stop pestering him; he could react with a kind of mock anger and let

her know she can't get what she wants through such "underhanded" ways; he could just give in; or he could set aside a time to discuss this with her.

Harry chose the fourth option. Appreciating how much this coat meant to Renee, he suggested that they find a special time to talk about it. She began by promising that she'd take care of it. "How can I know that?" Dad asked. "Do you remember the coat you left at the movies?" Renee answered that she could show her father that she was more mature now and able to take care of valuable things. Dad, still not entirely convinced, said, "Let's see how things go over the next three months. If you keep your word, we'll talk about it again."

Harry not only avoided a power play, but he also helped his daughter understand why she couldn't have the coat she wanted now. And Renee was better able to cope with the frustration because she thought of her own way to prove her maturity to her dad. A well-placed picture spurred a conversation that otherwise might not have taken place.

You can also establish a family ritual one night during the weekend—perhaps on Sunday, after the kids return from their activities. Rent a video and encourage your kids to invite their friends over. They'll like that—and it's a great way to meet their friends and come to know their world.

Do something very special together on holidays and summer vacations. You don't need to plan a trip to an exotic place, such as the Caribbean or the Sahara. Spending time at the shore or at a mountain lake or theme park will create memories your kids will treasure for the rest of their lives and give them lots more to talk about during those important times they carve out together.

Spending important moments to share thoughts and feelings, leaving notes for one another, and planning special activities together on holidays or vacations are some ideas families with limited time and busy schedules have come up with to help create a sense of connectedness. Maybe these are really good ideas for all families.

## "Did I Promise That?"

Naomi promised her son that she'd stop on the way home from work and pick up some chocolate ice cream for dessert.

Lydia told her daughter to stop whining, that she could have the doll she wanted to buy but she'd have to wait until Saturday.

Margot told her son that she'd be at his first Little League game of the season.

All of these women had good intentions, but none could keep her promise. Naomi had such a busy day at her office that she simply forgot. Lydia never really intended to take her daughter to buy the toy over the weekend—she simply didn't know how to say no so her daughter would stop whining. And Margot had to pack up and leave on an emergency business trip on the day of her son's game.

At one time or another, just about every parent has promised something he or she couldn't deliver. An occasional breach won't hurt. But when promises are broken time after time, your child can begin to react:

- He may feel that no one cares about him.
- He may come to believe that if he can't have something he wants right away, he will never have it at all.
- He may lose his trust in you. He'll come to believe that your words are empty and that you don't mean what you say.
- He may even come to believe this about other people as well.

There's another big problem in not keeping your promises: you may unwittingly send an unintended message—that promises don't have to be kept. Suppose you tell your son to clean his room, and he assures you he will do it tomorrow. Will he sense that he doesn't really have to follow through, even though he promised that he would?

Denise told me that from the time her child was two years old, she never made a promise she couldn't keep. If he asked to go to the zoo, and she couldn't go that day, she would promise to take him and promise to go as soon as she could. But she never promised a specific day, because "if something came up, he would be disappointed all over again." Denise added, "If he wanted something I didn't want him to have or to do something I didn't want him to do, I never said 'later' or 'another time' just to allay his whining. When I did promise something, he knew he could trust that I would really follow through."

This is not to say an occasional breach of promise will be devastating or create a lack of trust. Ten-year-old Vanessa's mom promised her that her friends could sleep over the coming weekend, but unfortunately Mom got called out of town. Mom explained to her daughter that she had every intention of having her friends that weekend, and why she couldn't honor her promise. Because her mom had been consistent about keeping her promises, Vanessa, while disappointed at this exception, understood that her mom didn't forget her and that she really did get called out of town. Vanessa came to appreciate that her mom has needs, too.

---

The world isn't a perfect place; your child doesn't expect it to be. And she doesn't expect you to be perfect either. But if you can keep your promises, at least most of the time, your child will likely keep her promises, too.

---

Sometimes we just plain forget. But to minimize the occasional forgetful episode, try to pay extra attention when talking to your child about something you promise to do. And don't promise something in the future if you have no intention of following through. If you really mean to say no, then say it—don't say "later" or "another time." And if you can't honor a promise because a business trip comes up or for any other reason, make sure to explain what happened and why and find a way to make it up to him.

The world isn't a perfect place; your child doesn't expect it to be. And she doesn't expect you to be perfect either. But if you can keep your promises, at least most of the time, your child will likely keep her promises, too.

## When Mom Says Yes but Dad Says No

Ten-year-old Marie knows her dad is very much against her having a computer in her room. She tries to convince him that he should reconsider his position by claiming, "Mom says I can."

Twelve-year-old Duane says, "Mom, John and the guys want me to go to the mall with them today." Knowing that his mom doesn't want him going to the mall without adult supervision, he quickly adds, "Dad already said I could go."

No matter how good a marriage you have or how closely your opinion echoes your spouse's, it's inevitable that you will disagree about some things. And when it comes to raising children, there are many areas that can be in contention: what to eat, when to go to sleep, what kinds of video games and movies are acceptable, whether they're old enough to have a sleepover at their friends' or have their own cell phone. What can you do when Mom says yes and Dad says no? In some families, one parent makes the final decisions. This "avoids tension," as one dad told me. But this strategy isn't perfect, as another father acknowledged: "Sometimes I let my wife make the decisions only to regret it. After seeing my son watching TV for two and three hours at a time, for instance, I feel I have to step in. 'But Mom lets me,' he wails. And that's when my wife and I end up arguing with each other."

Here are some other ways to deal with differences of opinion:

- Discuss with your spouse ahead of time what is acceptable for you regarding your child. If you feel strongly about one thing, then you may have to give in on another. For example, if you vehemently believe that your child shouldn't eat fast food, you may have to reconsider your policy of not having any sweets or favorite snacks in the house for him.
- If you don't have a chance to confer in advance or if your kids ask you about something you haven't even considered taking a position on, say, in a calm voice, "I'll have to talk to your dad about this first." This

gives you time to talk about the issue together and come to an agreement about how to handle it.

- If at all possible, try to involve your child in helping you come up with a compromise solution. This way, everyone feels satisfied. Marie, for instance, discussed the computer situation with her parents. She promised that if she could have a computer in her room, she would do her homework first and chat on the computer only with her friends and only when she has free time. With the added security of a block on unwanted chat rooms, Mom and Dad felt easier about having the computer. In time, they saw how responsibly Marie kept her word about doing her homework first.

You may decide that it's still unacceptable for your child to have a computer in his room. But involve him in the decision of where the computer could be placed as a compromise and how it could be used.

Duane's parents involved him in the decision about going to the mall. He told his mom, "If I can't go with the guys, they'll think I'm a nerd." His mom was surprised and flustered—she hadn't realized the reason for his intensity about this.

Still, she was determined to hold her ground. "Duane, you're too young, and I don't want to hear another word about it!"

To his credit, Duane came up with another idea. "You could come to the mall," he told his parents. "You can watch us but don't let on you're there." Mom and Dad could accept this solution—and Duane felt proud instead of angry and frustrated.

Another solution is to ask your child questions to gauge his readiness to be on his own at the mall. "What would you do if you got separated from your friends?" you can ask. "What if a stranger approaches you and asks for help?" Listen to your child's answers to determine whether or not you feel you can trust his judgment.

When you find yourself in a situation in which one parent says "yes" and the other "no," think about negotiation and compromise—and ask questions that help you decide what your child is ready for. When you think creatively as a family, a solution is often closer at hand than it may first appear to be.

# 14

# Sibling Rivalry

## Solving "Trivial" Problems

Children seem to have perfected the skill of getting all worked up over issues that seem nothing short of inconsequential: who gets first dibs on the slide in the playground, who gets the top bunk, who gets the biggest piece of pie, who gets the red pieces of candy. This often drives their parents crazy.

Here's a scenario that probably sounds familiar: it's Saturday afternoon and Dad is taking his two kids, aged nine and eleven, to the video store. Listen in:

**Haley:** You always get to sit in front. It's my turn to sit there.

**George:** No, it's *not*! You sat there last time.

**Haley:** No, I didn't. I remember you sat there last time when we went to the pool.

**Dad:** Come on, kids. Is it so important who sits in front?

It isn't important to Dad, but it is to Haley and George. In fact, it's so important that Haley's near tears and George is shouting at the top of his lungs. And the "discussion" will keep on escalating. Haley, according to her dad, has a perfect memory. She remembers what days her brother sat in the front seat, whether it was a long or a short trip, and where they went. Knowing her good memory, Dad believes she's probably telling the truth. At this point, completely exasperated, Dad feels like he needs to keep a scorecard: who sat where, when.

No matter how "trivial" an argument like this may seem to adults, it means the world to kids. They're arguing over territory, influence, and power. It's all terribly serious.

Dad doesn't know what to do. He just wishes they would be quiet. Maybe he should just pick one child to sit up front now and let the other one sit in the front seat on the way home. But that would be solving the problem for them, and he knows they'd probably never agree to that.

Here's how Dad learned to help his kids using problem solving. First, he acknowledged the importance to each child of sitting in the front.

> **Dad:** I know that sitting in front is important to both of you. Haley, how do you feel when you think George isn't being fair about this?
>
> **Haley:** Mad.
>
> **Dad:** George, how do you feel now?
>
> **George:** Mad.
>
> **Dad:** Can you two think of a way to solve this problem so you both won't be mad?
>
> **Haley:** I get two turns, and you get two turns next time. That's fair.

Both kids decided that this was a good solution. Knowing how each other feels is an important first step in solving a problem.

But often lessons have to be learned more than once. Last Halloween, Haley and George collected about three large bags of candy while out trick-or-treating. Of course they wanted to eat all of it. Mom and Dad agreed that they could each pick out twenty pieces from their own bags—and throw the rest away. They also limited the kids to one piece of candy a day. Both kids were OK with this, because, as Haley acknowledged, "We won't get stomachaches." George pulled out his twenty pieces of candy; Haley pulled out hers. Then she said, "George pulled out bigger pieces, so I get to pick five more." After Mom and Dad did all they could to keep from laughing, they agreed that Haley could pick out five different, but not five additional, pieces of candy.

You may wonder, as I did, why these parents didn't limit the amount of candy the kids could collect since they didn't let their kids eat it all;

throwing out bags of leftover candy seems like an awful waste. When I asked Haley and George's dad about this, he said, "The fun is the trick-or-treating. It's almost as if getting the candy is the excuse to enjoy dressing up in costumes and going around to different houses with friends. If we put a limit on the amount of candy the kids could eat, they'd only be able to go to one house, two at the most."

Another family deals with the issue of leftover candy in a very creative way: they conduct "the great candy weigh-in." Each bag of candy is weighed, and then each child receives a gift certificate to the local video store based on the weight of his or her bag. This way, the kids indulge in DVDs rather than chocolate. Yet another parent I consulted told me she just lets her kids eat as much candy as they want—for that one day. "It ends up not being so much," she says. "Their eyes are always bigger than their stomachs."

No matter what you do, there will always be too much candy. If you don't make a big deal of this and let your children help decide the best way to work this out, everyone will be happy.

However, for George and Haley, their clash over "trivial" problems doesn't stop with Halloween candy and riding in the front seat. When her brother doesn't take the dog out for a walk when it's his turn, even when the reason is legitimate (he's not home), Haley will do it but demands "credit." "He has to take him out two times in a row," she asserts with conviction. "Haley is like a bulldog lawyer," her dad told me. "She advocates for her side very strongly."

George has found some creative ways to counter Haley's rigidity. When he can't win by direct confrontation, he finds other ways to get what he wants. One afternoon, both George and Haley wanted to play a video game at the same time. George waited until she was distracted for a moment, and then planted himself firmly in the chair, refusing to budge.

But because Mom and Dad knew how to talk to their kids using the problem-solving approach, they asked both children what they considered "fair." In her inimitable way, Haley made a chart of who would have the chair and for how long. When George agreed to their "contract," the problem was solved.

It doesn't matter how the kids solve their problems. If both agree on the solution they choose and appreciate how the other person feels, they have learned important steps toward getting along with others. What better place to start than at home?

## "She Gets More Playdates Than Me!"

You come home from a hard day's work, expecting a big hug from your kids and eagerly anticipating a nice family dinner. But as soon as you put the key in the door, they run to greet you—not with a hug but with cascading complaints: "She has more crayons than me!" your younger child wails.

"Yeah, but he keeps breaking his and taking mine!" your oldest replies. Before you've had a chance to take off your coat, you're thrust in the middle of a pitched battle.

Many parents find sibling arguments hard to tolerate. They hate to hear their kids arguing continually and pointlessly; they hate to hear them arguing at all. In every parent's fantasy, siblings love and appreciate each other and work together harmoniously. But despite their love for each other, most siblings still find time and cause to fight, especially when it comes to the issue of who has "more."

"He has more toys than me!"
"He goes on more sleepovers than me!"
"She gets more playdates than me!"

You're probably tempted to take a logical approach when one of your kids voices a complaint like this. You may explain how the number of toys they each have is roughly equal. You may suggest that he play more with the toys he has. You may even become so exasperated that you say something like, "If you don't stop complaining, you won't have any toys at all!" When playdates and sleepovers come up, you may try to comfort your child by reminding him that he gets sleepovers and playdates, too, and even try to discuss the last one he had.

But comments like this, as well as logic, don't mean anything to a child who is feeling envious of or angry with his or her sibling.

The best way to address sibling rivalry over conflicts such as these is to help children redirect their focus so they're not thinking only about their brother or sister but about themselves. You can do this by asking your child a series of questions:

"What do you have that makes you feel really happy?"
"What activities do you really like to do?"
"What do you have that your brother [or sister] doesn't?"
"What do you do that your brother [or sister] doesn't?"

The first two questions help children focus on themselves—what they enjoy. This way, they're thinking about what they have and what's positive in their lives, as opposed to what they don't have or what's missing.

The last two questions help children separate from their siblings. When a four-year-old girl was asked what she has that her brother doesn't, she said, "My doll. I love my doll." An eight-year-old boy said, "I have my best friend, Eddie, and my brother doesn't."

Questions like these help children realize that they don't have to be envious of their brothers or sisters. They can learn to appreciate what they *do* have, instead of what they do not.

## Don't Play the Blame Game

Amy, nine, stubbed her toe on a chair as she came into the kitchen for dinner. "Ouch!" she whined. Seeing her brother standing nearby, she turned on him. "It's Mike's fault!" she cried. "He put the chair in my way!"

"I did not!" Mike said. "You blame me for everything."

Their parents exchanged looks: it was true—Amy always tended to blame others every time something went wrong.

Even now, Amy wasn't able to let Mike off the hook. "Just because you said that I won't let you listen to my new CD," she told him.

Mike's face grew bright red. Flustered and frustrated, he turned to their dad and said, "She's doing it again!"

But their dad was tired of being brought into this struggle. He'd heard it too many times. "Leave me out of it," he said. "You two work it out yourselves."

He was right that the siblings needed to work together to come to a solution. And he learned a new way he could help them do that. Here's how:

> **Dad:** Amy, how are you feeling right now?
>
> **Amy:** My toe hurts and I'm mad!
>
> **Dad** *(calmly)*: Mike, what can you say to your sister so she'll know that you didn't move the chair so that she'd get hurt?
>
> **Mike:** I know your toe hurts, Amy. I hate it when I stub my toe. But really, the chair is where it always is. Do you really think I moved it so it would be in your way?
>
> **Amy:** I guess not.

Amy wasn't happy, and she was still in pain, but she had to admit that her brother didn't do anything to hurt her; he hadn't really moved the chair. What enabled her to reach this conclusion was Mike's empathy. He told her that he knew that her toe hurt and that he had experienced the same hurt in the past. Only after talking about how she felt and how he felt about her pain did he bring up the fact that she was blaming him irrationally. And because Amy felt as if Mike was paying attention to how she felt, she was able to put her feelings aside and acknowledge the truth of what he said.

The same was true for Mike. He was able to talk to Amy in a calmer way because he'd felt supported by their father. When he asked, "What can you say to your sister so she'll know that you didn't move the chair?" he was implicitly telling Mike that he knew Mike hadn't set out to hurt Amy. With this support and his feelings acknowledged, Mike could let his anger fade and approach his sister in a way that she could hear him.

Blame can be assigned to anyone over any issue. Andrea, age nine, lost her favorite CD and told her parents that her eleven-year-old brother was playing it last—that he put it somewhere and now it's gone. Mom and Dad didn't know who had it last but talked to both of the kids this way:

> **Mom:** It seems that Andrea's CD is missing. I wonder how we can find it.
>
> **Andrea:** Terrell had it last, and he lost it.

**Terrell:** I did not. I put it back in the case.

**Andrea:** Well it's not there *now*!

**Mom:** Think hard. Where else could it be?

**Terrell:** I don't know. I put it back where it's supposed to be.

**Mom:** Andrea, did you look in the case?

**Andrea:** Yes. It's *not* there.

**Dad:** Let's look again.

The whole family went to look for the CD. Sure enough, the CD wasn't in the slot in front where Terrell said it would be. But when Mom kept looking, she found the CD in a slot near the back. Andrea had inadvertently put other CDs in the front, causing her favorite one to move to the back. Here's how Mom continued the conversation:

**Mom:** How do you think Terrell feels when you blame him before finding out what really happened?

**Andrea:** Mad.

**Mom:** And how do you really feel inside about that?

**Andrea:** Sad.

**Mom:** How do you feel now that you know Terrell didn't lose your CD?

**Andrea:** Embarrassed.

**Mom:** What can you do next time you think your brother did something before you find out what really happened?

**Andrea:** Well, for the CD, I could have looked harder for it first.

It's an important start. Andrea may think twice next time she wants to quickly blame her brother for something he didn't do.

Often, children who blame others for their problems do so because they crave attention, want to get their sibling in trouble, or believe that their siblings don't care enough about them to consider their feelings. It is also possible that children who blame others are just too proud to admit they were careless or made a mistake, perhaps out of a need to protect themselves from their own blame. If you can address those feelings first and acknowledge them—no matter how irrational—you'll probably find that, like Amy and Andrea, your children will be ready to talk about what might have really happened and to take responsibility for what happens to them.

## Stop Sibling Rivalry over Rules and Privileges

Four-year-old June complained that her ten-year-old sister gets to walk the dog by herself outside but she has to go with her mom. Like most parents, her mom tried to explain that when she's older, she'd be able to walk the dog alone, too, adding that it's not safe for her to be out alone, with or without the dog. But her mom might as well have saved her breath. This argument doesn't mean anything to most younger siblings. If anything, they might respond to it by saying, "I don't care about that. I know you love her more than me."

Six-year-old Dottie complains that her older brother Manny has more spending money than she does. Her mom tries to explain that Manny, who's eleven, gets more money because he's older and needs more things— and on top of that, he does chores for a neighbor Saturday mornings to earn some extra money. Her mom also explains that when he was Dottie's age, he received exactly the same amount of money she does now. She doesn't hear a word of her mom's explanation. "It's not fair!" she insists. "He always gets more than me!"

It's not just younger siblings who have trouble with this concept; sometimes older kids do, too. One afternoon, Manny asked his parents for some extra money. They explained that he'd already gotten his allowance and that he'd spent the extra money that he earned. "If you want more spending money," Mom explained, "you'll have to learn to save."

"You never say that to Dottie!" Manny cried. "You give her whatever she wants. It's because she's the baby. It's not fair!"

The issue of what's fair always arises with siblings. Although most parents try to be as fair as possible, inequities often arise. It's difficult for children to understand that fairness doesn't mean that everything has to be the same.

This is a hard concept for children to understand. How can you help them?

Involve them in considering why things are different for their brother or sister. For example, you could ask your younger child some questions:

"Why do you think your older sister can walk the dog by herself and you can't?"

"What might happen if you are out by yourself and the dog started to pull away from you?"

"How would you feel about that?"

"How do you think Mom and Dad would feel?"

You can ask your older child these questions:

"Why do you think we don't just give you everything you ask for?"

"What can you do so we will feel good about helping you out when you need something?"

By thinking about these questions, June, in time, came to understand that her older sister could hold on to the dog more easily than she could. She also thought about what might happen to the dog if it broke away.

When Manny answered questions about what he wanted, he realized that Dottie doesn't get everything she asks for and that he needed to learn to take responsibility for his allowance and his earnings. He decided to make a budget so he always had some money on hand.

Helping your children understand what they can and cannot do and have—and why the rules may appear to differ for a sibling—will help them appreciate that if they get what they need, they won't have to worry so much about being "fair."

## Sibling Spats: They're Not Always Bad

Have you ever heard, "He won't get out of the bathtub!" "She's wearing my jewelry!" "She won't get off the phone!"

I once asked a mom to make a list of what her kids fight about. She began—"Who goes first, who gets more attention, whose space it is, who gets more . . ."—but then she smiled and said, "A shorter list would be what they *don't* fight about."

The kinds of conflicts I talk about in this chapter—in addition to those I consider in previous chapters (losing at games in Chapter 2, jealousy in Chapter 6, and possessiveness in Chapter 8)—led me to ask what may appear to be a surprising question: are these types of conflict bad?

Unless your kids seriously hurt each other, physically or emotionally, conflicts between brothers and sisters are not only normal, but healthy.

As psychologists Deborah Vandell and Mark Bailey tell us, sibling rivalry is a fact of life. While friendships may end or be threatened by conflict, fighting with sibs is generally safe: you can't lose a brother or sister the same way you can lose a friend.

Normal conflicts give children an opportunity to learn about each other's wishes, needs, and thoughts. They can learn ways to oppose, disagree, and compromise. In other words, through conflicts like these, children learn to solve problems.

Let's take the example of Brad, ten, who accused his sister Debbie, eight, of cheating when she won a video game they were playing. Their mom took advantage of the conflict to ask Brad some questions:

"How are you feeling now?"
"How do you think your sister feels when you accuse her of cheating?"
"Does your sister really win all of the time?"
"What can you think of to say to Debbie so she won't feel mad or bad?"

By answering these questions, Brad realized that he did win sometimes and that if he continued to accuse his sister of cheating she may not want to play with him anymore. Brad learned to think about his own feelings and his sister's feelings, too.

Now let's look at Devon, whose little sister Kim kept "bugging" him every time he wanted to play with his friends, do his homework, organize his stamp collection, and, it seemed to him, anytime he wanted to get away from his sister.

The more Mom and Dad explained that Kim loves him and wants to play with him, the more agitated Devon became. One day, when Kim asked to go with him to the mall, Devon screamed, "Mom, tell Kim to get out of my hair. I want to be with my own friends! She's just a baby and a *girl*. And my friends will think I'm a dork if she tags along!"

Mom, feeling sorry for Kim, talked to both her kids the problem-solving way.

**Mom:** Kim, do you want to go to the mall with Devon or do you want him to play with you?

**Kim:** I want him to play with me.

**Mom:** Devon, how do you think Kim feels when you treat her like that?

**Devon:** Sad.

**Mom:** Kim, how can you find out what Devon might like to do, too?

**Kim:** Devon, could we play cowboys tonight? Just for a little while?

**Devon:** OK. But just for a little while.

---

Allowing your children to solve everyday problems at home, in a safe place, helps them practice the skills they will need to solve conflicts at school, in the neighborhood, and wherever they go.

---

Devon learned how to mesh his needs with the needs of his sister, and Kim learned to mesh her needs with his—planting the seeds for reciprocity and empathy later on. And while Kim didn't get to join her brother and his friends, she did learn how to be assertive without being aggressive.

Allowing your children to solve everyday problems at home, in a safe place, helps them practice the skills they will need to solve conflicts at school, in the neighborhood, and wherever they go.

# 15

# Peers

## "Mommy, No One Likes Me"

Billy, age four, sits on the sidelines while his friends play video games. Regina, age six, stands by herself during recess while the other girls flock together. Annette, age seven, comes home from school whining, "Jennifer won't play with me!"

Does your child spend too much time alone wishing he were part of the group? Does he pine to be included?

Wyndol Furman and Philip Robbins, and others who study childhood friendships, tell us that it's not the quantity of friends a child has that matters. Even if a child has only one or two good friends, that's all she needs to help her feel good about herself and others. But it's important to be able to form that friendship. Children who are rejected or ignored may end up feeling frustrated, angry, and sad.

Some children experience rejection the first time they ask to join in a game or invite someone to their house. Some children are naturally shy and don't know how to approach others. Some children don't know how to let other children know that they're interested in joining in. They may appear aloof, or even rejecting, and not realize it.

Grace, five, noticed some kids playing in the sandbox and ran over, enthusiastically shouting, "I want to play, too." The kids were very engrossed in building their sand castle and didn't even notice Grace. The children's well-meaning teacher tried to help by asking the kids if Grace could play, too. They let her into the sandbox but paid no attention to her.

The next day, when the girls were playing office, Grace couldn't figure out how to join in. That's because the day before, the teacher did the thinking for her. So she ended up sitting by herself again. Mom asked Grace a few questions to help her next time she wanted to enter a group already at play.

**Mom:** What did you do when you saw the girls playing office?
**Grace:** I told them I could be the secretary.
**Mom:** And what did they say?
**Grace:** We already have a secretary.
**Mom:** What could you have done to find that out?
**Grace:** Watched them play a while and see what they don't have.
**Mom:** Good thinking.

But Mom should be complimented, too. Researchers Kenneth Dodge and his colleagues have learned that kids who jump into groups without watching what the group is doing and don't wait for the right moment to enter are often rejected and not allowed in. Grace's mom helped her think about why she wasn't welcomed.

Here's another mom, talking with her daughter Annette about Jennifer, who wouldn't play with her. First her mom suggested, "Invite her to our house to play with your new video game."

The next day, Annette came home, again lamenting, "Jennifer won't play with me."

"Then let her come and ride your new bike," said Mom.

The next day, the same thing happened. "Mom," Annette whined, "Jennifer still won't play with me."

Finally, Mom asked, "What can you think of to do now?"

The next day, Annette came home beaming. "Mommy, Jennifer played with me today."

"What did you do?" asked Mom.

"I *asked* her."

Who was doing the thinking now?

With older children you can try a different technique. Nine-year-old Donna wanted desperately to make friends, but the more she reached out, the more she felt excluded. Donna's mother tried to help her by making the usual suggestions—but nothing seemed to work.

One day, she thought of a creative way to help her daughter learn to problem solve. She said to Donna, "I bet you can make up a story about a girl your age who moves into a neighborhood where she doesn't know anybody. At first she feels very left out. But after a few weeks, she found that she'd made many friends. How did that happen?"

Donna was fascinated by her mother's request. She'd never been asked to make up a story like this before! Here's the story she composed:

"Penny wanted to make friends but didn't know how. One day, she learned that another girl, Alice, loved horses. Penny also loved horses. Penny asked Alice if she wanted to go riding together, and Alice said yes. But the day they were supposed to go, Alice got sick and had to stay home. Penny visited her and brought her homework so Alice wouldn't fall behind at school. Alice thought that Penny was very nice to do that and liked her a lot. They became good friends and Alice introduced Penny to her other friends, and soon Penny had lots of friends."

Donna smiled when she was finished. She not only enjoyed the challenge of making up the story but also discovered that it was easier to think about how a fictitious child could make friends than it was for her to think about her own real situation.

Donna practiced using fictitious children a few more times. In time, she began noticing what her classmates liked to do. When she heard one of them say that she liked to go in-line skating, Donna said that she loved to skate, too, and suggested that maybe they could skate together one weekend. Donna was well on her way to making friends.

If we *ask* rather than tell our kids what to do, they can think of their own ways to solve their problems—if we let them.

## Help Children Appreciate Others' Tastes

Roger and Harris, both four, were playing together with their trucks. Roger wanted to play for a while with Harris's fire truck and offered his remote-control car in exchange. But Harris didn't want the remote-control car. Bewildered, Roger offered the car again and was again refused. Now he became agitated. It was his *favorite* toy. He couldn't believe that Harris didn't want to play with it. Within seconds, Roger dissolved in tears.

If you were to enter the room at this point, you probably wouldn't know what happened or why Roger was so upset. He just didn't understand that his taste doesn't always coincide with others. He feels bad that his special toy was rejected, and he was out of options—he counted on trading toys with Harris so he could get the fire truck he wanted. Now he doesn't know what to do.

Here's a game you can play to help children as young as four or five learn that different people like different things. Just as important, it helps them learn how to find out what another person likes.

It's called the "Do You Like?" game. Here's how Roger's mom played this game with her son and with Harris.

**Mom:** We're going to play a game. It's called the "Do You Like?" game. I'll start. Roger, *do you like* strawberries?

**Roger:** Yep!

**Mom:** Harris, *do you like* strawberries?

**Harris:** *(laughing)* Nope!

**Mom:** Do you two like the *same* thing or something *different?*

**Roger and Harris:** *(shouting out together)* Different!

**Mom:** Now, Roger, you try this game with Harris.

**Roger:** *Do you like* pizza?

**Harris:** Yep!

**Roger:** *Do you like* candy?

**Harris:** Yep!

**Roger:** *(getting carried away) Do you like* spinach?

**Harris:** *(giggling)* Nooooo.

Mom then asked Harris to take a turn asking Roger "do you like?" questions. They got so immersed in this, it was all she could do to stop them.

Once the questioning was done, Mom said, "Sometimes people like the *same* thing and sometimes they like something *different.* Is it OK for different people to like different things?"

The next time Harris didn't want to play with Roger's remote-control car, Roger showed him his action figure collection and asked, "*Do you like action figures?*"

Harris smiled and started playing with the figures. Mimicking the sound of a siren, Roger rolled Harris's fire truck around the room. Both kids were happy with their trade. And while Roger had learned that offering one of his toys in exchange for another's toy may get him what he wants, he also learned to appreciate that other people have wants and feelings, too.

You can play this game with your kids, too. If you only have one child, you can use a puppet, taking turns with your child speaking for the puppet. Feel free to ask about new categories, such as TV shows, movies, and pets, and let your kids make up new categories.

## "My Child Always Assumes the Worst"

Your ten-year-old daughter comes home from school distraught. "Lea didn't talk to me today," she says. "I know she's mad at me and doesn't want to be friends."

Your eight-year-old son hops in the car after Little League practice and says, "Graham bumped into me on purpose. And it really hurt. I'm never talking to him again."

Some children are quick to assume the worst. They jump to faulty conclusions about why people do the things they do.

Here's an example of how one dad used the problem-solving approach to help his daughter Sandy, engaging the help of her sister Molly.

**Sandy:** Dad, Lea's mad at me. She's supposed to be my best friend but she didn't talk to me all day. I asked her to play with me and she didn't even answer.

**Dad:** I know you're upset. Let's make up a story about a girl named Sherry who broke a playdate with her friend. See how many *different* reasons you and your sister can think of that would explain why Sherry might have done that.

**Sandy:** She didn't want to play with her anymore.

**Molly:** She felt sick.

**Sandy:** She was sad 'cause her dog died.

**Molly:** The teacher yelled at her.

**Dad:** Good thinking, girls. Sandy, now can you think of why else Lea might not have talked to you today?

**Sandy:** Maybe she got a bad grade on a test.

Thanks to this "why else?" dialogue, Sandy now realizes that there are many reasons Lea could have acted the way she did—reasons that have nothing to do with her.

It's especially important for children to understand this concept as they get older. Friendships become very important to preteens, and there are many opportunities for misunderstandings. For example, eleven-year-old Robbie lent his friend Todd his basketball and asked Todd to return it around dinnertime the following day. But Todd didn't show up. When Todd finally called, Robbie was very angry with him. "You said you'd come and then you didn't!" he said. "I'm never going to lend you anything of mine again!"

Todd waited for Robbie to calm down, and then said, "If you'd listen to me, I'll tell you what happened. I had extra homework and my mom made me stay home until I finished it. I'm calling you now to tell you I'll bring it to school tomorrow."

Though he was still angry that Todd hadn't called him sooner, Robbie understood Todd's predicament. More important, he also understood that Todd was just being thoughtless, not mean, as he had first assumed.

Here's another example of how one child found that things were not what they seemed to be. Jamie, age nine, was moping around the house because she'd just "broken up" with her best friend, Alison. When Jamie's mom asked what happened, Jamie said, "Alison promised to go to the movies with me on Saturday and now she says she can't go 'cause her mom is sick. I told her she's lying, and we got into a fight. Now she won't talk to me."

Jamie's mom asked, "How do you think Alison felt when you told her she was lying?"

Jamie paused. Clearly, she hadn't thought about that before. "I guess she was mad," she finally said.

"What can you do or say so Alison won't be mad and you can be friends again?" her mom asked.

Jamie thought for a moment and then said, "Maybe I should tell her I'm sorry."

Using the "what else?" phrase, her mom asked, "And *what else* can you think of to do or say?"

"I could ask her how her mom is feeling and say that when she's better, maybe Alison and I can go to the movies then."

By asking your child to consider other possible explanations for situations, or to back up and not jump to incorrect conclusions, she may learn to broaden her perspective. Children who blurt out in anger or just give up may end up jeopardizing important friendships.

## "My Child Brags Too Much"

Does your child need to exaggerate his accomplishments by telling other kids he does things you know aren't quite true? Does he put other kids down? Does he like to brag and show off to classmates about things he really is good at?

Raymond, ten, picked on girls shooting baskets at summer camp—he teased them whenever they tried to score, saying things like, "I could have made that shot with my eyes closed."

Kate, eight, told her friends that she won a medal in gymnastics at the gym she goes to on Saturdays—and made sure her classmates knew about it. Kate's mom tried to tell her that bragging this way would annoy her friends. But Kate's convinced that her friends will like her even more.

And Nora, age eleven, who got all As on her last report card, let her classmates know about that, too.

There are several ways to help children who brag too much. Raymond's mother said to him, "I want you to make up a story about a boy named Michael who brags a lot. I'll help you. First, you make up what Michael brags about."

"He says he can run faster than anyone at school," Raymond said.

"Now make up three reasons why Michael may want to brag," his mother said.

"Maybe he likes to be a big shot," Raymond said.

"Why else?"

"Maybe he thinks kids will want to be his friend. Maybe it makes him feel good inside."

"How do you think the other kids feel when Michael brags like that?" his mom asked.

"Probably mad," Raymond said.

"And how do you think Michael really feels inside when he brags?"

"Probably bad," Raymond said.

"What might his friends think if they run a race and Michael doesn't win?"

"They'll know he's a bragger," Raymond said.

"And what might happen if Michael keeps saying he's the fastest runner after the other kids know he isn't?"

"They won't like him," Raymond said.

"Can you think of a *different* way Michael could make friends and feel good inside?"

Raymond thought for a moment. "Maybe he could stop talking about how fast he can run."

At this point, Raymond's mother reminded him of how he always brags about what a good basketball shooter he is. Raymond thought of Michael and got the connection. "Yeah," he said, "I don't want to be like Michael."

One of the reasons kids like Raymond are able to make that connection is because using a made-up story about a fictitious kid enables them to look at the situation without feeling threatened. Talking about a make-believe child takes the heat off Raymond—he didn't have to be told kids might think he's a show-off or that he might not have any friends. Because he wasn't feeling stressed, he was relaxed enough to arrive at this important insight himself.

Kate's mom asked her what the kids said when she told them about her gymnastics medal. "My best friend said, 'I don't care,'" Kate said.

"And how did that make *you* feel?" asked Mom.

"Surprised," Kate answered. "I guess I can show it to her in a nicer way."

Nora's mom asked her daughter one important question: "What might the kids think if you get a B next time around?" Nora hadn't thought of that before.

It's one thing to feel proud of our accomplishments. It's another to exaggerate or flaunt them before others. Kids can learn that difference, too.

## Hobbies Can Help Kids Make Friends

The word *hobby* has an old-fashioned ring to it, but there's nothing dated about it. In fact, children who cultivate hobbies—who are interested in learning about something that's not directly connected to school—can reap many unexpected benefits.

Jay, twelve, told me how his special interest helped him make new friends. Since he was eight, Jay has enjoyed tap dancing, creating and performing his own dances to the Broadway musicals he has attended and loved. At home, he buys the CD or DVD and practices in his room for hours.

After he learns the dance, he makes props and stages a performance for his family. For several years, this was as public a performance as Jay felt comfortable staging. But at a school parents' night two years ago, Jay's mother, Loretta, met another mother whose son also liked to dance.

The moms encouraged their sons to get together to talk about their shared interest. Jay invited his new friend, Byron, over to visit and soon Byron asked if he could help Jay with his next "production."

It wasn't long before Byron brought his friends into the show, and then the group really began to grow. After about four months of rehearsal, they performed for the neighborhood at a community theater, selling tickets at two dollars a seat. With the money they raised, they bought a new supply of DVDs so they could learn new dances, they purchased materials for new props, and they set aside some funds for future publicity, such as posters announcing the next production.

In addition to the pure enjoyment Jay derives from dancing, his hobby has brought him many benefits. He used to be shy about revealing his unusual interest to other kids at school. But after meeting Byron, Jay began to feel safe about inviting other kids to his home. He's also learned how to balance dance time with homework because he knows that he practices best after his homework is done. He's learned some important entrepreneurship skills, like how to create and stick to a budget and how to market his skills. Best of all, he now has enough confidence to invite kids from school to attend his performances. To his surprise, they not only show up but want to join the group.

Today the group is so large that the kids have to take turns performing, building props, and organizing other behind-the-scenes activities for a production. Everyone pitches in.

Lee, twelve, found that her hobby helped her make friends, too. She loves to design bracelets and necklaces out of beads.

At first she made them for her grandma, her mom, and her sister. When she felt comfortable enough, she decided to make a bracelet for Nina, a new girl at the school she liked a lot. Although Lee didn't like the color purple, she noticed that Nina did. So Lee made the bracelet out of purple and white beads. When she gave it to Nina, the first thing Nina said was, "It's purple, my favorite color!" Not only did Lee's hobby help her make a new friend but observing the colors that Nina wore helped her become aware of what other people like—in this case a color that she wouldn't have chosen for herself. Recognizing that other people's feelings and preferences may differ from our own is an important skill in itself. When I asked Lee how she felt about making the bracelet, she answered with pride, "It made us both feel special because instead of buying something, I made something just for her. She liked it, and I felt good because I made it."

Your child doesn't have to have a unique talent or a special skill like Jay or Lee. It really doesn't matter what your child does. If he can find something important to him, he will put himself in a position to discover many more benefits and more pleasure than he can imagine. The fringe benefits of cultivating a hobby go beyond the pleasure of the activity itself.

■

# PART 4

# Building Life Skills

*Just as we can stretch our bodies for greater flexibility,
we can stretch our minds for greater possibilities.*

Are children who struggle academically so preoccupied with unresolved emotional issues that they can't focus on school? Or do children who have school-related problems lack the skills to keep up with their classmates, leaving them frustrated and uninterested and, in some cases, prone to acting out? Do creativity and the ability to "think outside the box" help children achieve greater success emotionally, socially, and intellectually?

How well your child does in school and in life depends on many interrelated factors, including his adeptness in social situations, how he behaves at home and at school, how motivated he is to achieve, and how well he actually performs.

In Parts 1 through 3, I talked about how unresolved problems can lead to behaviors that can interfere with academic success.

In Part 4, I will show you how learning skills related to solving problems can also have an impact on academic success—and how the two are intertwined. I will also suggest unique and creative ways to develop some of the very life skills that can help your child do well in school.

Take paying attention—a skill that requires listening. Have you ever found yourself talking with a friend, or your daughter, and suddenly realizing that you didn't hear a word she said? Or, answering a question you assume you heard but that wasn't actually posed? Or answering only part of a question while ignoring the rest? These situations have probably happened to all of us. But good listening is a critical skill to develop. I begin Part 4 by showing you how you can help your child fine-tune his listening skills while you fine-tune your own—in ways that can strengthen the bond between you and your child in important new ways.

Paying attention is one of the life skills that has been identified by researchers Karl Alexander, Doris Entwisle, and Susan Dauber of Johns Hopkins University as being important for academic achievement as early as the first grade. The others are learning to use time effectively, maintaining interest in the subject matter, and actively participating in the academic routine. In fact, according to another study of Entwisle and Alexander, the skills and work habits children have when they enter kindergarten are among the strongest predictors of academic motivation and performance throughout the elementary years.

Another life skill, responsibility, also contributes to success in school—and in life. Children first learn responsibility at home, as they see to their daily needs. As children grow, there are many ways to help them become responsible—you can ask them to do age-appropriate household chores, for example. But what can you say when they balk? Is it possible to stretch your child's attention span while teaching responsibility? How can you help your child welcome responsibility instead of flee from it?

You can also try giving your child a regular allowance. Or do you believe they have to earn money they receive, or that spending money should be contingent on good behavior? This is a complicated issue, and before you make a decision, you may want to consider the advantages and disadvantages of each option—and which strategies work best for your child.

What all children need to learn is to assume greater control over, and responsibility for, their schoolwork. Can children become excited about doing their homework? What unique role can dads play?

I'll also talk about how creativity and imagination can be added to the mix. Although we tend to think of these qualities as important to those who are drawn to music, art, or writing, they are in fact applicable to every field of endeavor. Arthur Cropley, in his classic contribution to the *Encyclopedia of Creativity*, writes, "creativity is . . . needed to achieve effective novelty in all areas: artistic, literary, and musical to be sure, but also in science, engineering, commerce, government, and interpersonal relations."

On a personal level, Cropley adds, "flexibility, openness, the ability to adapt the known or to see new ways of doing things, interest in the new, and courage in the face of the unexpected [can] . . . help the individual cope with the challenges of life, especially in the areas of change, uncertainty, adaptation, and the like, and they are closely connected with mental health."

I agree. To my way of thinking, spontaneity and flexibility of thought can relieve stress and anxiety about getting the right answer. Unquestionably, knowing the "right" answer is an integral part of certain lessons—for instance, two plus two is always four, and Harrisburg is the capital of Pennsylvania—but even math and geography aren't only black and white. In fact, rote learning has its limitations. Kids who only memorize facts may not know how to apply those facts to new situations in the real world, which may leave them unable to cope with unpredictable situations. In this section, you'll learn many creative and exciting ways kids can learn to play with numbers and learn state capitals—and nurture a love of reading the problem-solving way. Your child may even want to create his own stories and use all the skills you have given him on the way to becoming a thinking child.

# 16

# Listening

## Listening in School

Lenore got off the phone and was steaming mad. Her daughter Tara's second-grade teacher had just called to say that Tara had failed all three tests this week—math, spelling, and science—and science was her favorite subject.

The teacher sounded very frustrated. "Tara's a bright girl," she said. "She should be doing much better. In class, though, I notice she talks to her friend in the seat next to her when I'm trying to teach, and when I look at her notebook, it's full of doodles. And her homework is often incomplete and messy. I don't think she has a vision or hearing problem, and she doesn't have a learning disability. I just wish she'd get back on track."

After hearing this, Lenore walked to her daughter's room. "Your teacher just told me that you're wasting time in class, talking and doodling, while she's trying to teach," she said. "You're going to have to work harder. In fact, no playdates this weekend. You're going to get your homework done and I'm going to check it, and if it's not perfect you'll have to do it over."

"I don't have any homework!" Tara shouted.

"Don't talk back to me!" Lenore yelled back. "Do as I say or you'll be grounded all month!"

Tara turned her back on her mother. From her point of view, the conversation was over.

This wasn't the outcome Lenore had envisioned. Let's rewind the tape and begin differently. In this version, Lenore knocked on Tara's door and said, "Tara, your teacher tells me that you're failing tests, even in subjects you enjoy. What's happening?"

At first, Tara didn't want to talk about it, so she said, "I don't know."

Lenore was undaunted. "I bet if you think really hard, you'll remember what you were doing when your teacher was giving her science lesson."

Because Tara didn't feel attacked or threatened, she decided to answer honestly. "I like to talk to my friends, Mom," she said quietly.

"Tara," her mother began, "do you know what the word *proud* means?"

"Yeah, like when I do something good, like draw a horse."

"And do you know what the word *frustrated* means?"

"When I can't draw the horse good and it comes out all wrong."

"Now tell me how you feel when you fail a science test."

Tara saw the connection immediately. She smiled and replied, "Frustrated."

"And how do you feel when you pass your tests?"

"I feel proud," Tara blurted out.

Lenore then asked her daughter to think about what she could do to pass her tests.

"I could stop talking and doodling and listen better to the teacher," Tara said.

Now it was Lenore's turn to smile. "How do you think your teacher will feel then?"

"Proud," Tara said.

The next day, Tara came home from school beaming, "I told my teacher I'm going to make her *proud* and not *frustrated*."

But it wasn't only Tara's teacher who felt proud. Tara—and her mom—did, too.

## "Is Anybody Listening?"

Do you often feel that your kids don't hear you no matter what you say? Do you find yourself starting each conversation in a pleasant, calm, and quiet tone of voice, only to end up screaming at them at the top of your lungs? Are you going nuts because your kids never listen to you?

Here's a unique new way to change all that. It's a game I call "Silly Skits." Here's how one mom introduced it to her daughter Tamara and Tamara's friend Carla, both age eleven.

**Mom:** OK, kids, here's a little skit for you to read out loud. There's something silly going on here. See if you can tell what it is.

**Tamara:** My toes are red.

**Carla:** I got two pet turtles from my mom.

**Tamara:** I was out in the snow, and my toes got red.

**Carla:** They crawl funny.

**Tamara:** They itch.

**Carla:** One is really, really huge.

**Tamara:** Do you have some medicine?

**Carla:** It's green and slimy.

**Tamara:** Yucky! I don't like that medicine. I'll just soak my toes.

**Carla:** I'll get you some warm water to soak your toes.

**Tamara:** Thanks.

Both girls laughed their heads off. They knew it was silly because, as Tamara put it, "We were each talking about our own thing."

Mom then asked the girls to read the skit again, only this time, she instructed them to listen carefully for those places where one person *did* hear what the other was saying and to tap their knees when they heard it.

After they did that, Mom asked them a question: how can Carla let Tamara know that Carla really heard what Tamara said? "For example," Mom explained, "when Tamara says, 'My toes are red,' how can Carla let Tamara know that she heard the statement about her toes?"

"Carla can ask, 'Why are your toes red?'" the girls agreed. They then read the skit again, making up statements and questions that indicated that they were really listening.

Kids catch on to this game easily, and many enjoy making up their own silly skits. Here's one that Tamara and Carla made up:

**Tamara:** It's a shame about Keith's parents.

**Carla:** It's so hot.

**Tamara:** They got a divorce.

**Carla:** I wish there was a tree around here.

**Tamara:** Now he has to live with his mother.

**Carla:** Why does he have to live with his mother?

**Tamara:** Because his mother got custody of him.

**Carla:** Hey, there's the ice-cream man.

Mom was intrigued that the girls made up a silly skit about such a serious topic. She took the opportunity to ask how Tamara would feel if Carla *really* answered her this way. "I would think that Carla doesn't care about anybody but herself," Tamara said, an answer that indicated that she understood how important it is to listen to people.

If you use silly skits, you can remind your child of them the next time your child doesn't listen by simply asking, "Do you remember 'silly skits'? How can you answer me so I'll know you heard me?"

---

How can you answer me so I'll know you heard me?"

---

Your child will enjoy this exercise, and it will help her become a better listener without her even realizing it.

## "Do I Really Listen to My Child?"

What do you do when your child hits another or grabs a toy from a friend? Are you frustrated and exasperated because you've told him not to behave that way? Are you ready to lash out at him?

Adam, age four, tore up his father's cigarettes and threw them in the trash. Assuming it was a mistake, Dad didn't say anything. But when Adam did it a second time, Dad was furious. Threatening to spank Adam, he roared, "Never do that again!"

But when Adam's mom calmly asked her son why he destroyed the cigarettes, Adam answered, somewhat sheepishly, "Big Bird told me if we love someone who smokes, tell them to stop 'cause they'll die. Daddy, I love you and I don't want you to die."

Once he realized that what appeared to be Adam's misbehavior was really the boy's way of asking his father not to smoke, Dad was touched beyond words. "Son," he said, "I'll never smoke another cigarette again." He didn't. That was more than twenty years ago.

It doesn't matter what Big Bird might have really said. What did matter was how the boy interpreted it. Imagine how the boy might have felt inside had his dad not listened to him.

Sometimes we don't listen to our kids because we have an agenda, and some behaviors just trigger that agenda, no matter what may have precipitated it. For example, many parents want their children to learn to share. If they see their child grabbing another's toy, they may become so focused on teaching the value of sharing that they don't find out what's really happening in the moment from their child's point of view.

When four-year-old Ruby's mom saw her grabbing her doll from her friend who was visiting, Mom's first impulse was to shout, "*Why* did you do that?!"

Defensively, Ruby answered, "She's got my doll. It's mine."

Mom didn't really listen to the response; she was so intent on teaching Ruby to share that it really didn't matter to her what her daughter would have said. "When are you going to learn to share!" she demanded. "No one will want to play with you, and you won't have any friends. Now give back what you took!"

Ruby obliged. But how was she really feeling?

Here's how Ruby's mom handled this problem after she learned how to talk the problem-solving way.

**Mom:** What happened? What's the problem?
**Ruby:** She's got my doll. It's mine.
**Mom:** Why don't you want her to play with it?
**Ruby:** She keeps on playing with it and won't give it back.

Now Mom learned something she couldn't possibly have learned before—that from Ruby's point of view, she had shared her doll, and now she wanted it back. Instead of focusing on what she thought was the problem—not sharing—she focused on what Ruby saw as the problem—not getting her toy back after she did share. Now the nature of the problem was different, and Mom continued the dialogue this way:

**Mom:** What happened when you grabbed your doll?
**Ruby:** She kicked me.
**Mom:** Can you think of a *different* way to get your doll back so your friend won't kick you?
**Ruby:** We could play house.
**Mom:** That's one way. And if she says no, what else could you try?
**Ruby:** I could let her play with my [stuffed] animals.
**Mom:** Good thinking. You're a good problem solver. How do you feel when you solve problems so well?
**Ruby:** Proud.

Note that Mom ended this dialogue by saying, "Good thinking," not "good idea." Had she praised the idea itself, she could have inhibited Ruby from thinking about what to do in a similar situation. Let's say, for example, that on her next playdate, Ruby wants a toy her friend is playing with. She may remember that her mother said, "Good idea," when Ruby suggested that she offer her friend her stuffed animal. But suppose the girl didn't want the stuffed animal? Ruby might feel stymied as to what to do instead.

The point is that you want to encourage your child to be able to think creatively about solving problems as they arise. When you use the problem-solving way, you praise not *what* your child thinks but *that* your child thinks.

## Beyond Listening: Talking So Everyone Is Heard

Conflicts are normal—and inevitable. They occur in every family. But all too often conflicts arise because people misunderstand each other or misinterpret a remark. Here are some examples you may recognize.

Michelle, age ten, likes to wear tight pants and tops that don't match. When her mom asks her to change her clothes, Michelle snaps, "I know

what I'm doing! You think I don't know how I look? Leave me alone!"
Mom's upset because she wants her daughter to look her best and to learn
good judgment. She's also worried that the other kids will think Michelle
dresses strangely.

Here's what Michelle says. "My mom wants me to wear pants so big
they'll fall down—that way, they'll fit next year. But I don't want to wear
the same pants next year—they won't be in style, and my friends will notice that."

This is a classic miscommunication: Mom thinks that the kids will
tease Michelle because her pants are too tight, while Michelle's afraid that
the kids will notice if she wears the same clothes two years in a row.

Each thinks she has a legitimate concern. Each does not want to hear
what the other has to say.

Here's how the dialogue technique helped this mom and her daughter.

> **Mom:** Do we see this problem the *same* way or a *different* way?
> **Michelle:** A different way.
> **Mom:** I'm worried about what the kids will think when they see you
> dressed that way. Why is it so important to you to dress so your
> clothes are too tight and don't match?
> **Michelle:** Mom, it's the *in* thing. All the girls dress that way. I want to fit
> in.
> **Mom:** OK. You know what's going on in school.

But this kind of communication is not resolved easily. When we feel
strongly or concerned about something, it's difficult to hear an opposing
point of view. It is also difficult for our children. We can help them gain
insights into why they may be having a problem without criticizing them.
Michelle and her mom found that, although they made a start over the
clothes Michelle wears, they still needed more practice at listening to each
other. It wasn't long before they had that opportunity.

Michelle told her mom about a boy who has to be better than everyone else, who doesn't like her because she does better on tests than he does.
And what upsets Michelle the most is that this boy, who is quite popular,
ignores her. "But when I tell my mom about my problem," Michelle says,

"she says that maybe it's my fault: maybe I'm arrogant and boast about my grades. She always assumes it's my fault. So now if I have a problem, I tell her right before going to bed so she can't criticize me."

Mom is just trying to make sure that her daughter doesn't become a snob. She wants Michelle to know how she comes across to other kids. "I want her to understand why this boy may be ignoring her," Mom says, "so I can help her understand how people react." But Michelle interprets her mother's "help" as criticism and feels as if she's being blamed for being ignored.

After trying the dialogue technique, here's how Michelle and her mom were able to resolve this problem.

**Mom:** What makes you think the boy ignores you because you make better grades?

**Michelle:** He called me a show-off.

**Mom:** How do you think he knows you make better grades than he does?

**Michelle:** Maybe when he looked over my shoulder and saw it?

**Mom:** That's one possibility. Can you think of another?

**Michelle:** Maybe someone told him.

**Mom:** That's another possibility. Now think hard. Is there anything you might have done or said so he'd know you make better grades?

**Michelle:** Well, maybe the time I showed him my test. I made 100 on my math test, and I guess I wanted to impress him.

**Mom:** OK. Those are all possibilities. What do you think he might really have thought when you showed him the test?

**Michelle:** Maybe I was bragging?

**Mom:** What can you do now so he won't ignore you?

**Michelle:** *(pause)* Be friendly and stop bragging.

Mom was now able to help her daughter think about what it is that she may have been doing to cause the boy to ignore her. And by asking these questions in a genuine information-seeking tone of voice, Michelle felt more relaxed and was able to recognize the probable root of the problem. With Mom feeling no need to criticize any further, Michelle was less threatened and more likely to listen.

---

We often think our kids aren't listening to us. How often do our kids think no one is listening to them?

---

Miscommunication is common in many families. The first step is for parents and their kids to stop tuning each other out because they are all thinking only about their own points of view. As this mom learned to talk with her child the problem-solving way, she came to an important insight of her own. "Sometimes I think I'm listening to my child, but I don't always hear her." It's important for each to listen, really listen, so what's important to everyone can be heard. That's when true dialogue begins.

We often think our kids aren't listening to us. How often do our kids think no one is listening to them?

# 17

# Responsibility

## "Is the Middle of the Floor a Good Place for Your Toys?"

Your four-year-old leaves her toys wherever they happen to be when she's finished playing with them. You've explained that toys belong in her room. But she already knows that. You've told her a thousand times to put them away when she's done. And when she asks why, angrily you shout, "Because I said so!" or, "Don't make me ask you again!"

To relieve the toys-in-the-middle-of-the-floor annoyance, a neighbor suggests that you take your child to the store and let her pick out brightly colored stacking bins. You bring them home, set them up, and show her that her blocks can go in one, her markers in another, and her Legos in a third. But after two weeks the bins remain empty and her toys are still on the floor. Now you're completely exasperated. "If you don't put those toys away *now*," you find yourself screaming, "you won't *have* any toys!"

But of course this doesn't work, either. You just don't know what else to do.

Try helping your child think about why the middle of the floor isn't a good place for toys. Audrey, mother of six-year-old Shane, waited until she was feeling calm, and then asked her son an important question: "What might happen if you leave your trucks on the living room floor?"

Shane's first response was just to say, "I don't know."

Audrey didn't give up. "I bet if you think hard, you'll think of something," she said.

Shane tried again. "You won't let me play with them."

This is, indeed, a potential consequence, something that may happen next. But it wasn't the answer Audrey wanted. Parents who use the problem-solving approach try to help their children think of more empathic consequences, not just something that might happen to them. Audrey was tempted to tell him the answer she wanted to hear but resisted. Instead, she gently guided him in the direction she wanted him to go by asking another question: "What if Grandma comes to visit and she doesn't see your truck and keeps walking across the room?"

Prompted in this way, Shane said, "She might step on it and break it." Still not what Audrey was looking for, she continued: "And what else might happen?" Shane had to think about this. After a long pause, he looked at her and quietly said, "She might trip on it and fall down."

Now Shane thought about something he had never thought about before. Audrey continued:

"How might Grandma feel if that happened?"

"Mad," Shane answered, "and sad."

Now Audrey asked, "How would *you* feel if that happened?"

"Sad," Shane said, "and mad."

That's when Audrey asked, "What can you do now so that no one will fall and you won't end up feeling sad or mad?"

Questions like these help your child focus not only on how the other person will feel if she gets hurt but how *he* will feel if that happens. And this is what will probably motivate him to move his toys to a safe place.

When we threaten kids or explain consequences to them, kids usually tune out these demands, suggestions, and explanations. As early as age four, kids can answer questions that help them care about others while tuning in to their own feelings as well. You may never have to tell your child where to put his toys again.

# The Chore Wars

Does your child "forget" to take out the trash? Or does she insist she has too much homework to do the dishes? Maybe she leaves her clothes on the floor around her bed rather than putting them in the hamper.

How do you react? Originally, you assigned your child chores because you thought it was a good way to learn responsibility. That's how you learned it. You also needed some help around the house. But now wrangling about chores has become a real problem, creating tension every day; it's more of a nuisance than a help. How much easier it would be to just pick up the clothes or take out the trash yourself.

But that won't solve the underlying issue—and it certainly won't teach your child responsibility. Using the problem-solving approach, here are ways you can win the chore wars:

- Let your child choose a skill he can master—and start early. Four-year-old Benjamin loved to sort his socks and put them in their own special place in his drawer.
- Make sure that chores don't interfere with homework, time with friends, or other activities important to your child.
- Find out what's on your child's mind when she keeps "forgetting" to do her chores. Nine-year-old Gail thought that taking out the trash was a job for her brother. When her mother asked what she'd like to do instead, she said she'd set the table.
- Let your child plan ahead of time what she will do and when. This will give her structure, and she's more likely to complete those tasks she plans on her own. If time really doesn't permit a chore to be completed on a given day or at a given time, ask your child what she can do to solve the problem. For example, if she really does have a lot of difficult math homework that she wants to complete before she gets too tired, she can leave the dishes soaking in the sink until her math homework is done. She could also trade chores with her brother so that tonight she sets the table before dinner, and he does the dishes after dinner.
- Keep chores manageable. Telling your daughter to clean her very messy room may make her feel overwhelmed; she won't know where

to start. You can ask her what she'd like to do first, second, and third. That way she can decide to pick up her socks, straighten out her desk, and make her bed. Or you can ask her where she'd like to begin—with the corner by the window or the area nearest to her closet or door. In this way, kids still feel as if their room is their domain because they're the ones making decisions about what to put away and when to do so.

One mom felt hurt that her ten-year-old son Will kept "forgetting" to sort the laundry. She tried to keep her feelings to herself, but she eventually became so angry that she couldn't talk to her son without yelling at him— which aggravated their relationship and made her feel even worse. After learning to talk about feelings, Mom asked her son, "How do you think I feel when I come home and find the laundry still in the dryer?"

"Mad," answered Will. Then he paused. "I don't like sorting clothes, Mom," he admitted. "It's so . . . girlish. Can't I do something else?"

"What would you like to do?" Mom asked.

"Clear the table after dinner," Will said.

That conversation allowed Mom to understand her child's point of view, and Will came to understand hers. Importantly, Mom realized that her real goal was not to get the laundry sorted but for her son to learn responsibility.

Learning responsibility is an important life skill. Start early. Children who feel pride and a sense of accomplishment now will retain those feelings through adulthood.

## "Why Is My Child So Forgetful?"

Some children "forget" to do something because they really don't want to do it—perhaps such chores as throwing out the trash or cleaning their room. Others genuinely forget things they do want and need.

It seems inevitable—the day after you buy your child a brand new winter jacket, just the one he wanted, he ends up leaving it at school. Or the day before the big science test, she leaves her textbook in her locker. Some children borrow things from their friends—a dollar for a snack, a book to read, a pen—and forget to give it back until the other child calls and asks for it. Others forget to ask for money for the class trip, or forget about the class trip altogether.

We can explain that coats left at school can be stolen, that they can't study for their test if they don't have their books, or that their friends won't trust them if they don't return things they borrow. But most kids already know these things. When they hear us explain these things, they tune us out. And they still forget.

Perry's eleven-year-old son, Wynn, is so distractible that he puts food in the microwave, starts reading a magazine, and forgets that he was cooking. "When I go to use the microwave later in the evening, I find his soup still in there," Perry explains. "He talks with his friends and leaves library books at their house—and then he gets fined because he can't return them when they're due. I guess kids just can't multitask like we can," he added.

Carmen told me that her seven-year-old daughter, Monique, is more forgetful than Abbie, her five-year-old, and it may be because Monique has more on her mind—homework, after-school activities, decisions about who to call in the limited phone time available to her on school nights. Carmen began to think that she needed to spend more time helping Monique get organized but wasn't sure where to begin.

If these children sound like yours, here are some things you can do.

Instead of telling your child what might happen, pick a time when you have his attention and ask him: "*What might happen if . . .*

you forget your coat at school?"
you leave your books in your locker?"
you leave your library books at your friend's house?"
you forget to return things you borrow from a friend?"

Most children can think of consequences: their coat may get stolen, they won't be able to study for a test, they'll get fined if they don't return library books on time, they may lose their friends' trust if they don't return things they borrow.

If your child *can't* think of these things, you can guide her without telling her. For example, you can ask, "What might happen if someone you don't know sees your new coat and no one is looking?" "What might happen if you have a test and you don't have your books?"

Once your child has thought about potential consequences, you can ask, "How do you think you will feel if those things happen?" Once she tunes in to her own feelings, she'll be more open to solving the problem of forgetting. Rather than give her a suggestion, let her come up with an answer.

Now ask, "What can you do so you'll remember to bring home what you need [or to return what you borrow] next time?"

Victor, eight, who always forgot his books at school, said, "I can put a note on my locker that says 'Check today's homework assignment,' and 'See if I have any tests.'" Melanie, age ten, who often borrowed books from her friends and then forgot to return them, decided that she'd write a note to herself and write down the friend's name and day and time she'd return the books.

It may not work the first time or even the second. But when a child thinks of an idea himself, he's much more likely to carry it out than one suggested or demanded by us.

That's exactly what happened with five-year-old Riva, who frequently forgot to brush her teeth at night, especially if the cat or her sister followed her into the bathroom. They'd start playing or talking, and Riva would never even touch the toothpaste. When her mom asked Riva what she could do to remember her teeth, Riva said, "Put a picture of teeth on the mirror." Riva drew her own picture, and everyone was amused. The picture may be funny, but Riva doesn't forget about brushing anymore.

By letting your child come to his own thoughts and solutions, you've also changed the nature of the discussion. You're not focusing on what your child *forgets* but on how he can remember. Eventually, he'll come to feel proud of his own competence.

## "Do It Yourself!"

Does your child want you to pour his juice, put his toast in the toaster, cut his food, button his coat, and even pour ketchup on his burger? Does he tell you he can't do his homework before he even takes his books out of his backpack?

And how do you respond? Do you yell at him, "Do it yourself!" Or, tired of fighting and yelling, do you just capitulate and do it for him?

What many parents don't realize is that they created the problem themselves—by doing everything for their children when they were much younger. Children don't learn to be independent automatically; they have to be taught. Here's how Toby's parents helped him, when he was eight, to overcome his incessant dependence on them.

Instead of constant nagging or explaining why Toby should do things by himself, they made up a game called the "What Can I Do By Myself?" game.

First, they asked Toby to list three things he wanted his mom and dad to do for him. Assuring him that they'd be there to help him, they asked him to choose one item to try by himself. Toby said that he'd pour his own juice.

Toby approached this task slowly, first getting the juice from the fridge, then walking it over to the counter. "What if I spill something?" he asked—but because it was a game, he was smiling.

His parents, smiling too, watched him pour his juice with great deliberation. When he was done, he had a big smile on his face and enjoyed his juice immensely.

That evening, Toby asked his parents to pack his backpack. Instead of blurting out, "Do it yourself!" as they usually did, his parents reminded him of the game. With the mood now changed, Toby said, "Oh yeah, I can do it by myself."

Getting Toby to do his homework independently took a little longer, but it did happen. One day, Toby came home with a history assignment to find out biographical information about Abraham Lincoln. History was Toby's least favorite subject, and he balked. But Dad was ready with a good question: "Which of the following is true about Abraham Lincoln," he asked—"was he the tenth president of the American Cigar Company, the twelfth president of Puerto Rico, or the sixteenth president of the United States?"

Toby laughed because he knew the answer and beamed, "The sixteenth president of the United States!"

Seeing that Toby was excited, Dad asked, "What were some important things he did while he was president? You can look it up on the computer."

"Can you do that for me, Dad?" Toby asked. But then he smiled. "Oh yeah," he said, "I can do it myself." Dad stayed with his son while he searched for the information, and then they discussed what they had read together. After that, Toby was able to complete the assignment by himself.

Some children always rely on their parents to keep track of their things, which they frequently misplace. If this sounds like your child, try to make her more self-reliant by asking, "Where were you playing with your doll today?" If that doesn't lead her to her lost doll, ask, "Where else were you playing with your doll?" If that fails, too, ask, "Can you think of something to do now until I can help you find your doll?"

A child as young as four might answer, "I can draw with crayons." That's your cue to say, "You're a good problem solver." Even though she hasn't yet found her doll, she is learning that you are not always at her beck and call. And while she waits, she may remember where her doll is all on her own.

To help our children learn independence, we must not make them overly dependent on us. And the seeds of that independence can be planted as early as preschool. Praise new skills, encourage your kids to practice them, and let them know it's OK to make mistakes. Children who have the emotional strength to tackle life's daily hurdles now are less likely to fear future challenges.

## Should I Give My Child an Allowance?

When I was a kid, my parents gave me a set weekly allowance based on my age, not on what I did or didn't do around the house. Some parents link payment to household chores. And some parents don't give their children any allowance at all. Instead, they give their kids money for what they want, within reason, providing they do what they're supposed to.

Each option has its pros and cons. Here are some things to think about as you decide how to handle the allowance question.

If you decide to set a weekly allowance:

- Children can save for what they want, learn to manage money, and plan ahead
- They may stop nagging you for money since they know how much they're getting and when they will get it

*However*, when your child wants something more expensive, you may end up giving her the extra money she needs. And you may believe your child is getting money for nothing—that it teaches money comes too easily.

If you give your children money for chores (cleaning their rooms, helping with the dishes, folding the laundry), they will:

- Learn to value money
- Understand that money has to be earned
- Be less likely to spend their money frivolously
- Develop a greater sense of responsibility

*However*, you may resent paying children for routine chores that they should be performing simply for being members of the family. In addition, children who get paid for household chores may come to think only of themselves and not of the needs of the family; they do chores only to get paid—the wrong reason.

If money is contingent on good behavior:

- Children may be better behaved
- Children may perceive money as something to be earned, as they do if they are paid for chores

*However*, children's good behavior is based on an external reward, not a genuine desire to behave.

What do kids have to say about all this?

Regarding the weekly allowance, Alicia, nine, thinks saving money helps her with math. "I add and subtract what I have saved and decide how much I can spend," she explains. Twelve-year-old Kelly sees the benefits of saving: "Saving my own money helps me think more about how much I really want something," she explained. But Danette is afraid to spend her money because, "If I spend it now, something newer and more expensive will come along that I want more." And eight-year-old Gary adds, "But I can't spend it on anything that will 'destroy my mind.'" This means he can't buy music CDs that preach hate or violent video games, even if he's saved up enough money to buy them. "But that's OK," he added. "I can still get stuff I want."

Edward, ten, who gets paid for weekly chores, says he doesn't care if he has to do extra chores to save for something special. "I'm just grateful to have it at all," he admits.

Eleven-year-old Marcy's mom follows the third option, giving her daughter money for snacks at school and going to the movies with her friends—but only when she does what she's supposed to do, which is to clean her room, do her homework, and stay out of trouble at school. Her mom explained that of course she wouldn't withhold money for a little infraction. But, she explained, if Marcy had to be reminded "time after time" to do the dishes, then she wouldn't give Marcy money when she asked for it.

I asked Marcy how she felt about that, and she said, "I try to make sure I do things right. I don't want to ask my mom for money and have her say, 'Not this time. You don't deserve to go see this movie because you were forgetful with your chores.'"

If you withhold money occasionally, it won't do any harm. My own feeling is that monetary rewards or the threat of punishment should not be the primary force that drives kids to "do things right."

Ten-year-olds Kendra and Felicia get their weekly money differently: they earn points by doing something special around the house or for getting to school or bed on time. They think it's a good idea. "You don't feel guilty about getting money for no reason," Kendra explains, adding, "I save my money. Mom and Dad want me to be responsible."

For Danette, who is afraid to spend money she saves, perhaps being given money for the little things she wants may be a good option—at least for a while. That way, she can feel free to spend the money she has and slowly work her way up to feeling safe to spend some of her savings.

There is no absolute right or wrong way to handle money issues with your children. What matters is not how you give money to your kids but how your kids value and spend the money they get.

# School, Homework, and Learning

## Who Does the Homework?

Your daughter brings home a math assignment so difficult she can't begin to puzzle it out. She asks you for help—she wants you to do it for her.

Your son put off finishing his book report and now he's in a crunch. He asks if you can help him with just one small part. Should you agree to do so, just so it will be done?

If you're like many parents, you're very tempted to help. According to researcher Christine Nord, parents who are involved in their child's schooling have children who do better in school. But before jumping in to help with homework, you have to stop and think about what kind of involvement is helpful. If you do your child's homework for him, what will he really be learning?

Stop for a moment and consider your goal. Maybe it's not so much to help him complete the task as to entice him to throw himself into the task with renewed energy and vigor. There are many creative ways to do this.

If your child says homework is boring, you can spice it up. Let him help you cook dinner while you discuss the difference between one-quarter teaspoon and one-half teaspoon. If your child is very young, you can place two apples on the left side of a table and two on the right side and let her count them. Let your child choose other objects to place on the table. If she is learning to subtract, take some of the objects away and let her count the ones that are left. You can apply the problem-solving vocabulary used in social situations to non–social type content by asking questions like, "Is the answer to 1 plus 2 the *same* as 1 plus 1 plus 1 or is it *different*?" "How are a train and a car the *same*? How are they *different*?" You can make these combinations of numbers or classifications as complex as your child can absorb. Here are some other ideas.

You can combine specific skills, like arithmetic, with feeling words by asking:

> "Would you feel *happier* with 1 [show one finger] piece of pizza or 2 [show two fingers] pieces?"
>
> "Would you feel *happier* if you could buy 1 pint or 1 quart or 1 gallon of your favorite ice cream?"
>
> "Would you feel more *frustrated* if you needed 5 dollars for something you wanted to buy and you had 100 pennies, 5 dimes, 36 nickels, and 7 quarters, or if you had 200 pennies, 11 dimes, and 2 quarters?"
>
> "Which would make you feel most *proud*: learning to play the violin well in 3 years, 51 weeks; 3 years, 14 months; 3 years, 371 days; or 4 years, 1 month?"

You can also make up games about other school subjects. If, for example, your child is studying geography, you can ask, "Which city does *not* belong in this list—and why not? Springfield, Harrisburg, Albany, Philadelphia." To tap into historical knowledge, you can ask, "List three presidents who served *after* 1950 and one who served *before* that year." Again, you can make these questions as challenging as your child needs them to be to hold his interest.

Any subject the child is studying can be turned into an exercise using the skills of problem solving. Take the idea of consequences, one of the cornerstones of the problem-solving approach, and apply it to social studies by asking: "*What might have happened if . . .*

> Washington's soldiers did not listen to him while they were crossing the Delaware?"

Martin Luther King Jr. had not been assassinated?"
cities didn't have a government?"

Or discuss Martin Luther King Jr.'s civil rights plan through the problem-solving lens by asking:

"What was his goal?"
"What were the steps he took to reach that goal?"
"What obstacles got in the way of reaching that goal?"
"How did he get around those obstacles? What new steps did he take?"
"How long did it take to accomplish those steps?"
"What can a civil rights leader do today to continue trying to reach that goal?"

One way parents and their kids enjoy thinking about math and other subjects in school is based on the popular Memory Game. When you were a kid you probably had cards with animals or objects that you placed facedown, turning them over two at a time hoping to find a match. You can adapt this game by making index cards to create a deck that reflects the content your child is learning in school. But instead of creating duplicate cards, create pairs of cards that test your child's knowledge. For instance, if your child is studying the multiplication table, make a card that says "12" and one that says "4 × 3." When he turns those over, it's a match. Or make up a deck that tests knowledge of state capitals, so that "Harrisburg" will be the match for "Pennsylvania." You can do this with any subject your child needs to master.

One boy, age nine, loved playing games like these so much that he tackled his homework with new enthusiasm. Feeling challenged and proud, he didn't want to ask his parents for help; he wanted to master it himself.

When you're creative, you encourage your child to be creative. By guiding but not doing your child's homework, an activity so important in his day-to-day life, you're showing him that you care—enabling him to care, too. But you're also showing him that you have faith in him to find a way to complete the task on his own.

# Homework: When to Do It

The homework wars. They erupt in so many households. Parents remind children of their assignments, then nag. Children whine and procrastinate. Many times, it's bedtime and your child's homework is still incomplete, or perhaps not even begun. How do you handle it?

Here's what happened when one mom, Louise, used demands and threats with seven-year-old Darnell.

**Mom:** Darnell, you've been home from school for nearly an hour and you haven't even begun your homework. No TV and no friends over until it's done.

**Darnell:** But Mom, I'll *do* it!

**Mom:** We go through this every day. I want it done *now*. If you don't, you won't get it done at all and your teacher will be angry, and you'll fall behind in school.

The trouble was that Louise was talking *at* Darnell, not to him. Here's how she learned to involve her son using the problem-solving approach.

**Mom:** Darnell, what subjects do you have for homework tonight?

**Darnell:** Spelling words, math, and science.

**Mom:** Which do you want to do first?

**Darnell:** I guess my words.

**Mom:** Good. Do you want to work on your words *before* or *after* your snack?

**Darnell:** After.

**Mom:** OK—and what will you do *after* you finish your words?

**Darnell:** Play outside.

**Mom:** OK—and will you do your math *before* or *after* dinner?

**Darnell:** Before.

**Mom:** And science?

**Darnell:** After.

**Mom:** Darnell, I'm very proud of you. You made your own plan.

This is a good start. Once your child starts thinking of his own plan, as Darnell did, you can ask some additional questions, such as:

"How long do you think your math will take?"
"What will you do if it turns out you need more time?"
"What will you say or do if your friend calls while you're in the middle of your math homework?"

And, if your child is old enough to tell time:

"At what time will you begin the next subject?"

Children as young as seven love to make their own plans. That way, they feel involved in the planning process and committed to the outcome.

Older children need to make plans for more complex tasks. Amelia, age eleven, had a report on a historical event due in two weeks, and it was her style to wait until the night before to begin reading the book. And the more her mother nagged her to start earlier, the more Amelia resisted. Mom tried a different tack by asking these questions:

"When is your report due?"
"How many days do you have to do it?"
"What's the first thing you have to do?"
"How long do you think that will take?"
"Then what do you have to do?"
"How long do you think that will take?"

Dividing more complex tasks into smaller steps, leaving enough time for each step, can help reduce stress and the sense of being overwhelmed. Amelia realized she had to do some research on her topic, chose both the Internet and the library, estimated how long each would take and how long it would take to actually write up her report. Using a calendar, she counted the days she estimated for each step and figured in time for the rest of her homework and other activities. With practice, she got better at all this with each assignment and soon had her short- and long-range projects completed in time to get a good night's sleep before they were due. With a little effort, and guidance from you, your child can get skilled at this, too.

When your child is able to plan his time, whether for short- or long-term projects, he will feel more in control while learning about responsibility, organization, and time management. Not only will he probably enjoy school more, but he can rely on these skills for the rest of his life.

## Nurture a Love of Reading

Even when children are too young to read, they can love books. If you have a preschooler and you read to her, she loves the tone of your voice, the expressions on your face, the attention you give her. And she hears the words and sees the pictures. Research has shown that this combination of emotional warmth and exposure to books helps very young children bond to you, learn to love reading, and achieve success once they're at school.

Following are some ways you can excite your kids about books.

Let your child pick out books he wants to "read." Just going together to the library or the bookstore and browsing through the selection creates an important bonding time for you and your child.

When you make your selections, read the whole story through without interruption so your child can see where the story is going. Then, read the book again as a problem solver. Ask your child how each of the characters felt when something happened to them. Then ask, "Have you ever felt that way?" If there's an illustration showing a character's feelings, let your child point to it and make a "sad" or "angry" or "happy" face himself. Then ask him how another character in the story could make that character feel better.

For example, in Judith Viorst's classic children's book *Alexander and the Terrible, Horrible, No Good, Very Bad Day*, Alexander's mom took him to the dentist and the dentist found a cavity. You can ask your child how Alexander felt about that, whether your child feels the *same* way or a *different* way about going to the dentist, and why he feels the way he does. You might also learn what's on your child's mind by asking, "What are some things that would make you feel you would be having a terrible, horrible, no good, very bad day?"

For stories that involve conflicts between siblings or friends, or a child and his parents—as many stories for preschoolers do—you can reread the story and stop at various points to help your child think about how the characters feel, how the problem could be solved, and how events might relate to events in her own life. Ask questions like these:

"How did the children in the story solve their problem?"
"Do you think that was a good way to solve it? Why or why not?"
"Can you think of other ways the kids could have solved their prob-
lems?"
"What might happen if they used your idea to solve the problem?"

The Berenstain Bears books are excellent springboards for discussion about people's feelings and how to solve problems. For example, in their book *The Berenstain Bears Get into a Fight*, Brother and Sister Bear are sitting on their deck with their backs to each other, not talking, because they had an argument. After asking the above questions, you can ask your child if anything like that has happened to her, how she felt, how she thinks the other child might have felt, and how she did, or could, solve the problem.

In addition to the questions you can ask your prereader, you can also stretch your older child's thinking with stories he enjoys by asking questions like:

"Why do you think the girl in the book acts that way?"
"Why else might she act that way?"
"Is there anyone in your school who acts that way?"
"Why do you think she does?"
"Why else might she act that way?"
"Can you think of something to do or say so she won't act that way?"

If anything happens in the story that happened to you when you were young, share your memories, thoughts, and feelings with your child. When eleven-year-old Maura, for instance, read the Harry Potter books, she and her mother ended up having a long discussion about what it means to be an orphan, about their own families, and how lucky they feel to have each other.

As your children grow and learn to read on their own, don't give up your reading time together—instead, allow it to evolve. Now you can take turns reading to each other, for example. (The truth is, many older children still love being read to.)

Taking the time to read with your child shows him that you value reading as an activity. Using books to jump-start discussions helps you to learn important and intimate things about each other that you might not otherwise have learned.

Another way to nurture a love of reading is to encourage your child to use books as a springboard to make up stories of his own. You can begin by guiding him to invent a different ending to the story he just read as a way to help him look at the story from the perspective of different characters. And by doing this, your child can think about how he would feel if he were in the situation depicted in the book. Loving stories that other people write may inspire your child to create his own—giving him the opportunity to organize his thoughts and feelings about what's important to him. If he wants to, he can read his story to the family—a safe way to let you know what's on his mind. But creating his own stories also gives him the opportunity to think about, organize, and express his views to the most important audience of all—himself.

## Use Sports to Teach Math

Do you and your kids share an interest in football or baseball? Maybe soccer, basketball, or hockey is more appealing to you. Sports can be a wonderful way to get your kids as excited about math as they are about points, runs, or goals.

I thought of this idea when I visited a fifth-grade class in which many children were doing poorly in math. It was in 1983, the year the Philadelphia 76ers won the basketball championship. The kids had been up all night celebrating. They told me more statistics about each player, including the bench players, than I would ever know or remember—including not only how many points each player scored in the final game but also each player's season average. Astonished by their knowledge, I thought to myself, "Who says these kids can't learn?"

After they settled down, I asked them questions about math that included feeling words, an important part of the problem-solving approach, but I adapted my questions to suit the 76ers: "Would you be *happier* if the 76ers won by 8 times 5 minus 20 points, or 8 times 4 plus 16 minus 6 points?" I also added fun ways to play with numbers with the "more than one way" concept, also part of the problem-solving approach. For example, with a basket scoring either 2 or 3 points and a free throw after a foul scoring 1 point, I asked how many ways the 76ers could score a total of 6 points. I wrote questions like these on the board, divided the class into small groups, and asked them to solve the problems together. They didn't get all the answers right, but their excitement and enthusiasm never abated. Even the teacher couldn't believe it. And from that day on, after their teacher adapted many of his lessons to sports, most of the students improved in math.

If you and your child enjoy football, you can apply this interest in math by saying, "There are five ways a team can score points." Ask your child to name as many as he can and how many points are scored each way. If she doesn't know them all, then pool your knowledge until you come up with all five:

- Score a touchdown = 6 points
- Extra point (kicking the ball through the goalposts after a touchdown) = 1 point
- Conversion play after a touchdown (passing or running the ball into the end zone from the two-yard line) = 2 points

So a touchdown can result in 6, 7, or 8 points.

- Safety (when an opponent with the ball is tackled in his own end zone) = 2 points
- Field goal (when the ball is kicked through the goalposts instead of going for a touchdown) = 3 points

Once your child understands the scoring, introduce a new game. Start with a simple question: "If a team scored a touchdown and an extra point, then separately, a field goal, how many points would the team have?" (*Answer: 10.*)

Then ask, "How many ways, within the rules of the game, can a team score 9 points?"

Three possibilities are (1) a touchdown and a field goal, (2) three field goals, (3) one touchdown with the extra point and one safety. Your child may even think of an extremely rare situation of three safeties and a field goal. However, if he offers three conversions and a field goal, which also totals 9 points, that is incorrect because unlike safeties, conversions cannot be scored independent of a touchdown.

Now make this harder for your older kids. Ask, "Suppose your team is losing the game by 16 points. How many ways can your team tie the game?"

Answers include (1) a touchdown plus an extra point plus three field goals, (2) two touchdowns, each with a 2-point conversion, (3) two touchdowns, each with an extra point, and a safety, or (4) a touchdown with a 2-point conversion, two field goals, and a safety. Of course, this scoring sequence is unlikely, but it will stretch your child's thinking. While inconceivable, it's even possible within the rules of the game to make 16 points with eight safeties.

Make up your own combinations and encourage your kids to make up questions of their own. You may want to do this at dinner or at halftime. If baseball is your game, you can ask questions such as: "How many ways can a team score 2 runs in one at bat?" "Can you think of rare ways, such as a pitcher throwing a wild pitch, a balk, or the other team making an error?"

Kids love thinking about ways teams can score. Each game you watch together will take on a whole new twist. And math may end up being more fun, too.

## Dads: An Important Ingredient of Academic Success

When it comes to succeeding in school, dads seem to make a big difference. A survey of more than twenty thousand children, reported by Christine Nord, suggests that regardless of income, parental education, race, and ethnic group, children whose fathers are involved in their education earn more As, participate in more extracurricular activities, enjoy school more, and are less likely to repeat a grade. This is equally true for boys and girls.

Researchers can't say for sure why Dad's involvement is such an important ingredient in academic success. It may be that children want to achieve to please their fathers and, in turn, themselves. It may also be that the time spent together adds an extra bond between father and child. Mom's involvement in school is of course important. But when you have Mom plus Dad, the combination is dynamic.

Researchers have shown that dads who get involved in other areas of their children's lives from the very beginning are more likely to get involved with their school and schoolwork, too. Here are some special ways dads can make their presence known and appreciated in their kids' schools:

- Stop by the school, even if only occasionally, and volunteer to help out. Even spending a half hour in your child's classroom or on the playground at recess can have a huge impact on your child's school performance.
- Make something for the classroom—a bulletin board, for example.
- Volunteer to tutor a child who needs help.
- Volunteer to accompany your child's class on a field trip.
- Speak with your child's teacher about how you can help your child in specific ways in terms of her academic, social, and emotional development.

You'll experience great rewards if you are able to follow up on any of these suggestions. First, you'll know more about what your child is learning in school. You'll also meet your child's friends. Finally, with all the specific information you've picked up from seeing your child in her academic environment, interacting with the teacher and her peers, you will be in a better position to help your child plan realistic goals and how to reach them.

How can dads get involved with their child's homework? Many dads I spoke with check their child's homework to make sure it's done, and they show any errors to their child to do again. While that is showing their children they care, an important ingredient in itself, other dads do a bit more.

Several told me how they take their children through the steps to complete math or science projects. As one dad said, "My son has to slow down. He wants the answer right away, and if he doesn't see it, he wants me to just tell him. So I ask him to walk me through the problem—  it gets him thinking about what he's doing. Like with equations, I'll take him through the first step or two, just to get him started. It changes his pace." This dad helps his child think about how to plan and complete science projects as well. He talks to him about what materials he'll need, helps him think about when and where to get them, what he has to think about next, and so on. He then added, "If I gave him the answers, not only would he not learn how to find them, but he wouldn't feel the pleasure and pride that he does when he discovers the answers himself."

Another dad helps his ten-year-old daughter, Gwendolyn, with her math homework by reviewing formulas with her and helping her apply them to problems. During one such session, Gwendolyn spontaneously started playing teacher, explaining these rules and steps to a group of imaginary friends. Proudly, she explained, "Since I'm the smartest, I teach them what Dad teaches me. I give them names. When I can't explain something, I ask Dad to teach me again. Then I explain it again to 'Dumbo' until he can do it. That makes me feel smart." I asked Gwendolyn how this helps her. "When I teach 'Dumbo,'" she said, smiling, "I have to slow down and be patient. And I can learn at my own pace. No tests, no stress." I then asked her if it helps her with her real homework, and she answered, "It helps me enjoy math more. And I made a new friend, too, who was having trouble with her homework. After I rehearsed with my imaginary friends, I could teach my real friend."

---

"If I gave him the answers, not only would he not learn how to find them, but he wouldn't feel the pleasure and pride that he does when he discovers the answers himself."

---

Beatrice Wright, now an adult, reflected on how her dad had an impact when she was growing up. "Mom was there all the time, but when Dad got involved, it was special. He often seemed so tired and worn out when he came home from work. But he always made it fun when we sat down together to go over my homework. He would ask me questions about what we were studying, and I had to look up information in the encyclopedia or the dictionary (we didn't have computers in those days). And after ten or fifteen minutes of doing homework together, he seemed to come alive again—he had renewed energy."

All the dads I talked with had that kind of energy, and it showed.

There are lots of ways dads can get involved in their children's education. I've suggested some, but there are many more. In reality, it doesn't matter what you do. It's *how* you do it. The more involved dads are, the more involved their children are. Everyone benefits.

# Epilogue

I hope I have shown you how to help your children cope with feelings, become more competent, develop healthy relationships at home and at school, and learn important life skills for future success. As you thoughtfully weigh *your* options each day, deciding how to handle situations that arise, your children can learn to weigh *their* options as well. In today's complicated world, more than ever, we must not only give our children skills they need to make good decisions in life—but also the freedom to use them.

I would love to know interesting stories and vignettes that come up in your family. You can write to me at:

Department of Psychology
Drexel University
245 N. 15th Street MS 626
Philadelphia, PA 19102

You can also contact me by phone at 215-762-7205, by e-mail at mshure@drexel.edu, or through my website at www.thinkingchild.com. I'd love to hear from you.

# References

## A Message for You

Shure, M. B. *Interpersonal Problem Solving and Prevention: A Five-Year Longitudinal Study, Kindergarten Through Grade 4.* #MH-40871. Washington, DC: National Institute of Mental Health, 1993.

Shure, M. B., and B. Aberson. "Enhancing the Process of Resilience Through Effective Thinking." In *Handbook of Resilience in Children*, S. Goldstein and R. Brooks, eds. New York: Kluwer, 2005.

Shure, M. B., and G. Spivack. "Interpersonal Problem-Solving in Young Children: A Cognitive Approach to Prevention." *American Journal of Community Psychology* 10 (1982):341–356.

## Chapter 1

Ginsburg, H., and S. Opper. *Piaget's Theory of Intellectual Development: An Introduction.* Englewood Cliffs, NJ: Prentice-Hall, 1969.

## Chapter 2

Brooks, R., and S. Goldstein. *Raising Resilient Children.* New York: McGraw-Hill, 2002.

Gallwey, W. T. *The Inner Game of Tennis*, rev. ed., p. 116. New York: Random House, 1997.

McFarlane, E., and J. Saywell. *If . . . (Questions for the Game of Life).* New York: Villard, 1995.

# Chapter 3

Carter, G. R. *Back to Basics: Social and Emotional Health.* Jan. 2002. Monthly newsletter, Association for Supervision and Curriculum Development. Also available online at www.ascd.org.

Casbarro, J. *Test Anxiety and What You Can Do About It.* Port Chester, NY: National Professional Resources, Inc., 2003.

Elias, M. "Prepare Children for the Tests of Life, Not a Life of Tests." *Education Week*, September 26, 2001, p. 40.

Huffman, L. C., S. L. Mehlinger, and A. S. Kerivan. "Risk Factors for Academic and Behavioral Problems at the Beginning of School." Report of the Child Mental Health Foundations and Agencies Network, 2000. www.nimh.nih.gov.

Williams, M., and W. Linguvic. *Body Change: The 21-Day Fitness Program for Changing Your Body . . . and Changing Your Life!* Carlsbad, CA: Mountain Movers, 2001.

# Chapter 4

Danziger, P. *Amber Brown Goes Fourth.* New York: Putnam, 1995.

Hetherington, E. M., and J. Kelly. *For Better or for Worse: Divorce Reconsidered.* New York: W. W. Norton, 2002.

Krasny, L., and M. Brown. *When Dinosaurs Die.* New York: Little, Brown, 1998.

Mellonie, B., and R. Ingpen. *Lifetimes: The Beautiful Way to Explain Death to Children.* New York: Bantam, 1983.

Roeper, A., and I. E. Sigel. "Finding the Clue to Children's Thought Processes." In *The Young Child: Review of Research*, W. W. Hartup and N. L. Smothergill, eds., pp. 77–95. Washington, DC: National Association for the Education of Young Children, 1967.

# Chapter 5

Baldwin, C. P., and A. L. Baldwin. "Children's Judgments of Kindness." *Child Development* 41 (1970):29–47.

Grief, E. B. "Sex Differences in Parent-Child Conversations." *Women's Studies International Quarterly* 3 (1980):253–258.

Koch, J. "Gender Issues in the Classroom." In *Handbook of Psychology*, vol. 5, W. M. Reynolds and G. E. Miller, eds., pp. 259–281. Hoboken, NJ: Wiley, 2003.

Newberger, E. H. *The Men They Will Become: The Nature and Nurture of Male Character.* Cambridge, MA: Perseus, 1999.

Newcombe, N. "Gender Differences." Interview, *Talking About Kids*. WHYY-FM, Philadelphia, PA, March 19, 1998.

Pollack, W. *Real Boys: Rescuing Our Sons from the Myths of Boyhood.* New York: Random House, 1998.

Ruble, D. N., and C. L. Martin. "Gender Development." In *Handbook of Child Psychology: Social, Emotional, and Personality Development*, vol. 3, N. Eisenberg, ed., pp. 933–1016. New York: Wiley, 1998.

Shure, M. B. "Fairness, Generosity, and Selfishness: The Naïve Psychology of Children and Adults." *Child Development* 39 (1968):875–886.

# Chapter 6

Eisenberg, N. *The Caring Child.* Cambridge, MA: Harvard University Press, 1992.

Light, P. *The Development of Social Sensitivity.* New York: Cambridge University Press, 1979.

Nowicki, S., and M. P. Duke. "The Association of Children's Nonverbal Decoding Abilities with Their Popularity, Locus of Control, and Academic Achievement." *Journal of Genetic Psychology* 153 (1982):385–393.

Roedell, W. C., R. G. Slaby, and H. B. Robinson. *Social Development in Young Children.* Monterey, CA: Brooks/Cole, 1977.

Spivack, G., J. J. Platt, and M. B. Shure. *The Problem Solving Approach to Adjustment.* San Francisco: Jossey-Bass, 1976.

# Part 2 Introduction

Brennan, P., J. Hall, W. Bor, J. M. Najman, and G. Williams. "Integrating Biological and Social Processes in Relation to Early-Onset Persistent Aggression in Boys and Girls." *Developmental Psychology* 39 (2003):309–323.

Crick, N. R., M. A. Bigbee, and C. Howes. "Gender Differences in Children's Normative Beliefs about Aggression: How Do I Hurt Thee? Let Me Count the Ways." *Child Development* 67 (1996):1003–1014.

Crick, N. R., J. F. Casas, and M. Mosher. "Relational and Overt Aggression in Preschool." *Developmental Psychology* 33 (1997):579–588.

Hoover, J. H. "Bullies Beware." *Education Week*, May 28,1997.

Nansel, T., M. Overpeck, R. S. Pilla, J. Ruan, B. Simons-Morton, and P. Scheidt. "Bullying Behaviors Among U.S. Youth: Prevalence and Association with Psychosocial Adjustment." *Journal of the American Medical Association* 285 (2001):2094–2100.

Smith, P., M. Singer, H. Hoel, and C. L. Cooper. "Victimization in the School and the Workplace: Are There Any Links?" *British Journal of Psychology* 94 (2003):175–188.

Stattin, H., and M. Kerr. "Parental Monitoring: A Reinterpretation." *Child Development* 71 (2000):1072–1085 (1083–1084).

# Chapter 9

Hamilton, C. *Momisms: What She Says and What She Really Means.* Kansas City, MO: Andrews McMeel Publishing, 2002.

# Chapter 10

Gershoff, E. T. "Corporal Punishment by Parents and Associated Child Behaviors and Experiences: A Meta-Analytic and Theoretical Review." *Psychological Bulletin* 128 (2002):539–579.

Straus, M. "Spanking and the Making of a Violent Society." *Pediatrics* 98 (1996):837–842.

# Chapter 11

Ladd, G. "Having Friends, Keeping Friends, Making Friends, and Being Liked by Peers in the Classroom: Predictors of Children's Early School Adjustment." *Child Development* 61 (1990):1081–1100.

# Chapter 12

Berenstain, S., and J. Berenstain. *The Berenstain Bears' New Neighbors*. New York: Random House, 1994.

Centers for Disease Control and Prevention, National Household Survey on Drug Abuse. In D. P. Crockett, "Critical Issues Facing Children in the 2000s." *Communique* 31 (February 2003):10.

Heusmann, L. R., J. Moise-Titus, C. Podolski, and L. D. Eron. "Longitudinal Relations Between Children's Exposure to TV Violence and Their Aggressive and Violent Behavior in Young Adulthood: 1977–1992." *Developmental Psychology* 39 (2003):201–221.

Hoyt-Goldsmith, D. *Celebrating Ramadan*. New York: Holiday House, 2001.

National Campaign to Prevent Teen Pregnancy Report. In *14 and Younger: The Sexual Behavior of Young Adolescents* (summary), B. Albert, S. Brown, and C. Flanigan, eds. Washington, DC: National Campaign to Prevent Teen Pregnancy, 2003. Also available online at www.teenpregnancy.org.

National Household Survey on Drug Abuse. Office of Applied Studies. Washington, DC: Substance Abuse and Mental Health Services Administration, 2001.

National Youth Tobacco Survey. "Tobacco Use Among Middle and High School Students, United States, 1999." *Morbidity and Mortality Weekly Report*. Washington, DC: U.S. Department of Health and Human Services, January 2000.

Office of Juvenile Justice and Delinquency Prevention Report. In D. Prothrow-Stith, "Girls: The Third Wave of Youth Violence." *The Challenge Newsletter* 10, no. 4 (June 2002). Also available online at www.thechallenge.org.

Shure, M. "I Can Problem Solve (ICPS): An Interpersonal Cognitive Problem Solving Program for Children." In *Innovative Mental Health Programs for Children: Programs That Work*, L. A. Reddy and S. Pfeiffer, eds., pp. 3–14. Binghamton, NY: Haworth, 2001.

# Part 3 Introduction

Katz, L. F., L. Kramer, and J. Gottman. "Conflict and Emotions in Marital, Sibling, and Peer Relationships." In *Conflict in Child and Adolescent*

*Development*, C. U. Shantz and W. W. Hartup, eds., pp. 122–149. New York: Cambridge University Press, 1992.

Parker, J. G., and S. R. Asher. "Peer Relations and Later Personal Adjustment: Are Low-Accepted Children at Risk?" *Psychological Bulletin* 102 (1987):357–389.

Vandell, D. W., and M. D. Bailey. "Conflicts Between Siblings." In *Conflict in Child and Adolescent Development*, C. U. Shantz and W. W. Hartup, eds., pp. 242–269. New York: Cambridge University Press, 1992.

Witkin, G. *KidStress: What It Is, How It Feels, How to Help*. New York: Viking, 1999.

# Chapter 14

Vandell, D. W., and M. D. Bailey. "Conflicts Between Siblings." In *Conflict in Child and Adolescent Development*, C. U. Shantz and W. W. Hartup, eds., pp. 242–269. New York: Cambridge University Press, 1992.

# Chapter 15

Dodge, K., D. C. Schlundt, I. Schocken, and J. D. Delugach. "Social Competence and Children's Sociometric Status: The Role of Peer Group Entry Strategies." *Merrill-Palmer Quarterly* 29 (1983):309–336.

Furman, W., and P. Robbins. "What's the Point? Issues in the Selection of Treatment Objectives." In *Children's Peer Relations: Issues in Assessment and Intervention*, B. H. Schneider, K. H. Rubin, and J. E. Ledingham, eds., pp. 41–54. New York: Springer-Verlag, 1985.

# Part 4 Introduction

Alexander, K. L., D. R. Entwisle, and S. L. Dauber. "First-Grade Classroom Behavior: Its Short- and Long-Term Consequences for School Performance." *Child Development* 64 (1993):801–814.

Cropley, A. "Creativity." In *Encyclopedia of Creativity*, vol. 1, M. A. Runco and S. R. Pritzker, eds., pp. 629–642 (631). San Diego, CA: Academic Press, 1999.

Entwisle, D. R., and K. L. Alexander. "Entry into School: The Beginning School Transition and Educational Stratification in the United States." *Annual Review of Sociology* 19 (1993):401–423.

# Chapter 18

Berenstain, S., and J. Berenstain. *The Berenstain Bears Get into a Fight*. New York: Random House, 1982.

Nord, C. W. *Father Involvement in Schools*. Champaign, IL: ERIC Clearinghouse on Elementary and Early Childhood Education. ERIC Document Reproduction Service No. ED 419632, 1998.

Viorst, J. *Alexander and the Terrible, Horrible, No Good, Very Bad Day*. New York: Scholastic, 1972.

# Index

# About the Author

**Myrna B. Shure, PhD,** a developmental psychologist at Drexel University in Philadelphia, is the creator of the "I Can Problem Solve" (ICPS) program—a school-based social and emotional learning/violence prevention program published by Research Press. The ICPS program has been recognized for research and service by numerous national organizations, including the Office of Juvenile Justice and Delinquency Prevention (OJJDP); the National Association of School Psychologists (NASP); the Center for the Study of Prevention of Violence, University of Colorado; the U.S. Department of Education; and the Collaborative for Academic, Social, and Emotional Learning (CASEL). It is also included in the National Registry of Evidence-Based Programs and Practices (NREPP). Dr. Shure is author of the *Raising a Thinking Child Workbook,* an ICPS program for families, also published by Research Press, with recognition by the Strengthening America's Families Project, the OJJDP, and NASP. She has been recognized by the American Psychological Association's Psychology Matters initiative for research relating to schools and families resulting in valuable applications that make a difference in people's lives. Her books for parents, *Raising a Thinking Child* and *Raising a Thinking Preteen* are both Parent Choice Award winners. Dr. Shure offers workshops nationwide and is also a media consultant on issues of mental health in our nation's youth.

The following is a list of books by Myrna B. Shure.

## For Families

*Raising a Thinking Child: Help Your Young Child to Resolve Everyday Problems and Get Along with Others.* New York: Henry Holt, 1994. Paperback, Pocketbooks, 1996.

*Raising a Thinking Child Workbook.* Champaign, IL: Research Press, 2000.

*Raising a Thinking Preteen.* New York: Henry Holt, 2000. Paperback, Owl, 2001.

# For Schools

*I Can Problem Solve (ICPS): An Interpersonal Cognitive Problem Solving Program* [Preschool]. Champaign, IL: Research Press, 1992.

*I Can Problem Solve (ICPS): An Interpersonal Cognitive Problem Solving Program* [Kindergarten/Primary Grades]. Champaign, IL: Research Press, 1992.

*I Can Problem Solve (ICPS): An Interpersonal Cognitive Problem Solving Program* [Intermediate Elementary Grades]. Champaign, IL: Research Press, 1992.